also by Shannon Guerra

Upside Down: Understanding and Supporting Attachment in Adoptive and Foster Families

Oh My Soul: Encountering God in Honest, Unconventional (and Sometimes Messy) Prayer

Work That God Sees: Prayerful Motherhood in the Midst of the Overwhelm

the *ABIDE* series:

Rest in the Running
Hope in the Waiting
Clarity in the Longing
Bravery for the Next Step
Obedience to Move Forward
Surrender to Win

risk the ocean

an adoptive mom's memoir of sinking and sanctification

shannon guerra

Copyright © 2023 Shannon Guerra

All rights reserved. No part of this book may be reproduced in any form or by any electronic or mechanical means, including information storage and retrieval systems, without permission in writing from the publisher, except by reviewers, who may quote brief passages in a review.

ISBN 978-1-7360844-9-6
ISBN (ebook) 979-8-9887158-0-1

Scripture quotations are from the ESV® Bible (The Holy Bible, English Standard Version®), copyright © 2001 by Crossway, a publishing ministry of Good News Publishers. Used by permission. All rights reserved.

Portions of scripture in **bold** are the author's emphasis.

The events and conversations in this book have been set down to the best of the author's ability, although some names and details have been changed to protect the privacy of individuals.

Cover design by Copperlight Wood
Cover image by Abhishek Fodikar via Unsplash

Printed and bound in the United States of America

Published by Copperlight Wood
P.O. Box 298086
Wasilla, AK 99629

www.copperlightwood.com

Praise for *Risk the Ocean*

Risk the Ocean is deeply personal, theologically rich, and full of encouragement and hope for anyone who has followed God into a storm of epic proportions. As a fellow adoptive mother, Shannon's stories of difficulty and attachment disorders made me feel seen in a way that few others have accomplished. I will be sharing this book with many friends, and may I suggest that you grab one for your church library as well? The adoptive families in your midst will be thankful and blessed.

– Natasha Metzler, author of *Pain Redeemed*

Few mothers craft their lives with ink and grace; even fewer serve the Great Commission while mothering. In *Risk the Ocean*, Shannon shares her raw testimony: her journey as a brand new idealistic adoptive mom to a seasoned fortress of strength and perseverance-with-joy. Integrity beams up and out of it on every page. This book will reshape how you parent your children, adopted or not.

– Katie James, author of Tetragon Lift

Risk the Ocean is a breath of fresh air as Shannon gracefully acknowledges the myriad of emotions that bubble to the surface (or burst through the dam) when we say "yes" to adoption. This book is not the neatly packaged "bless your heart" version that often pairs well with these stories, but instead this vulnerable account portrays the beautiful, messy, chaotically redemptive version. In her no nonsense way, she gently calls us to rise and reside in this sacred space: trusting, hoping, and believing in his plan for his children, piece by piece, and peace by peace.

– Jess Ronne, executive director of The Lucas Project and author of *Sunlight Burning at Midnight*

This book is incredible, not just because the content is so close to my heart but also because Shannon is such a great writer. The rhythm and way she leads the readers through is beautiful, almost like poetry; Shannon speaks with humility and authority as she shares her story. Painful yet honest truth flows through the pages, displaying that hard is not bad.

– Lacey Steel, director of Cultivate Relationships

Shannon's spiritual insights are delivered with a refreshingly raw transparency rarely found in today's Christian publications, affording the reader a front-row seat to God's immeasurable love and grace toward us. From beginning to end, her personal journey from darkness into God's glorious light confirms the message of the gospel. While *Risk the Ocean* may be of particular interest to adoptive families of children with special needs, the author's spiritual journey through hardship, grief, sanctification, and healing is highly relatable and anyone fortunate enough to read the pages of this book will come away encouraged and more equipped to press on toward the goal for the prize of the upward call of God in Christ Jesus.

– Maggie Montgomery, author of Gethsemane Road

This is the book to read if you are looking into adoption. Shannon pulls back the "amazing" and "wonderful" curtain that society has placed on adoptive families to reveal the true day-to-day struggles, failures, mistakes, and seemingly imperceptible wins. From regression to detachment, Shannon vulnerably shares the blood, sweat, and tears that real sacrificial love requires. As an adoptive parent, I finally felt heard, understood, and even cared for.

– Nathan Steel, director of Cultivate Relationships and author *UnLove* for Nathan and Lacey,

who know the path

contents

note from the author / 1

1: stretch marks / 3

2: to see the forest through the trees / 17

3: heavy wind / 29

4: fighting phantoms / 39

5: let it break / 49

6: the underwear strikes back / 63

7: on the same side / 77

8: make them scour the anchor / 91

9: scar tissue / 103

10: conduit / 113

11: wild poetry / 125

12: just keep it together / 137

13: a path which few can tell / 149

14: teamwork / 161

15: curveball / 173

16: the space between two joys / 187

17: how we bake bread / 199

18: where breakthrough comes from / 211

19: the long view / 223

postscript: the cost / 237

Man dreams and desires;
God broods and wills and quickens.
When a man dreams his own dream,
he is the sport of his dream;
when Another gives it to him,
that Other is able to fulfill it.

  - George MacDonald, *Lilith*

note from the author

This isn't a story about adoption. I meant for it to be, though.

Every time I tried writing it – dozens of times – I tried to make it about adoption because that's what I thought it was supposed to be about.

But I was wrong.

And it turns out, *that* is what this story is about: Me being wrong. Me, doing a lot of the right things but sometimes in the wrong ways. And also, doing the right things but feeling like they must have been the wrong things because they didn't seem to work out as neatly or as fast as I thought they should.

So mostly, this is a story about learning to be okay with the process of obeying and learning and growing and surrendering and being imperfect – otherwise known as sanctification – because His perfection is enough.

For over ten years I wrestled with trying to figure out if this was about me and my kids, or cultural adjustment and family transition, or secondary trauma or depression, or something else entirely.

And the answer was finally Yes. Yes, it was about all those things. But also No, because it was also about something else entirely: It was about me and Jesus.

It was about coming to the realization that He calls us to these things so we will empty ourselves of our us-ness that cannot do what needs to be done, because He wants to fill us with His Him-ness that does everything.

That is the only way we meet Him on the surface of the water without sinking.

1: stretch marks

If you lived in southcentral Alaska in the fall of 2012 you might remember we had record-breaking rainfall that year, collecting in every hollow and cavity it could find. From roughly Seward to Talkeetna, creeks and rivers burst at the seams, spilling everywhere. Roads and bridges washed out and flooded, and many neighborhoods were unrecognizable, including ours.

But it wasn't just outside. The inside of our three-bedroom house in Wasilla was also unrecognizable, and not just because the crawlspace flooded again.

After a night of messes from both a child and a cat puking, two poopy pull-ups, and less than four hours of sleep, I dried Reagan off after her third shower in 36 hours and hugged her, telling her for both of our sakes that I loved her...that I also liked her...and that we were going to get through this. She couldn't possibly understand what the words meant, but I prayed she understood my tone.

The same day, Andrey ran up to me, clinging and crying, "Ma-moh! Ma-moh!!" He'd hit his head, and I kissed him and prayed for his owie. A small grin emerged as he experienced something new: Finally, a ma-moh to comfort him.

The distance between that day and the next, like all of those early days, seemed like a space of years elapsing. So much happened in each span of twenty-four hours. I was stretched, Vince was stretched, the kids were stretched. Our coffee pot started making funny sounds from overuse. I think I started making funny sounds from overuse, too.

My first journal entry as a mother of six, including two new six-year-olds, started with this heading:

```
Tuesday, Sept. 3, 2012 - I think it's the
3rd, at least.

We are all home. Eight of us, together.
It is hard, not romantic, not warm and fuz-
zy. Here is my comfort zone:
```

I drew a small rectangle in the middle of the page.

```
And here is where God has planted us:
```

I drew an arrow to the edge of the page, as far as it could go.

```
And it is difficult. I am learning to
love when I don't feel it, to smile when
I'm irritated, to wipe a 6-year-old's bot-
tom with as much grace as I can muster
because it's not her fault she was aban-
doned at an orphanage that did not nurture
her past this.

I know it is for great good. And I knew
the attacks would come because the future
of these kids is at stake. And I know He is
protecting us and our other children be-
cause He has their futures in mind, too. It
is all for our good. For all of us. And our
comfort zone will expand to meet our cur-
rent location - His love is deep and wide,
and He will stretch our tent pegs.
```

I've read that entry many times since then and wondered if it was true. I mean, I know parts of it were true – God was protecting us, yes; it was all for great good, yes.

But my idea of God having everyone's futures in mind was, I now know, very different from what He actually had in mind. All of our futures were at stake, including those not yet born. And yes, those futures were still *good*, but they were also complicated, and utilized a different definition of "good" from what I expected or had ever imagined.

Let me go back. A month earlier we were in Bulgaria, completing final adoption requirements to bring our new son and daughter home. We checked in to one of the same hotels we had used in March when we first met Andrey and Reagan. I slept a little, woke up jittery at 3 am, ate some cold leftover pizza, and went back to bed for a few hours.

When I woke up for good, the sky was clear and blazing, lighting up the buildings on the terraced city.

We were ready to storm the castle. This was the day God declared freedom to the captive, joy for mourning, beauty for ashes, and copious amounts of caffeine for the jet-lagged and exhausted.

We drove to the village outside of town to pick up Reagan, feeling déjà vu laced with adrenaline. Minutes ticked by as we waited for someone to answer the door at the orphanage. Leaves rustled. A grey cat wove through the bushes nearby; a stork sat on the roof of a building across the alley.

The door finally opened and we were ushered into the same room we had interviewed in five months earlier, with the same director of the orphanage – and this time, she spoke to us in English. We smiled. *Thought so.*

We signed papers we couldn't read that were verbally translated for us, just like in March, but this time we walked out of the building with our daughter. It was shockingly undramatic – no fireworks, the sky didn't change color, birds didn't erupt from trees. We just added a child to our family and the world went on like nothing happened.

We had a ninety-kilometer drive to make and Reagan was quiet the whole time. Just watching, staring out the windows, looking at everything we passed. Sunflower fields changed to corn fields, which changed to a city we recognized from our previous trip and an orphanage we vividly remembered. Same paperwork, same matter-of-fact meeting, same lack of drama. But Andrey was all smiles for us.

Two castles stormed, two children redeemed. For good, forever.

Neither of them were upset in the slightest about leaving. No tears, no anxiety, no emotions whatsoever about saying goodbye to the places they had lived in for years. Neither of them had bonded with anyone. It's easy to misinterpret this as good news, but months of pre-adoption training told us that since they hadn't bonded with anyone in the past, it would be harder for them to bond with anyone in the future. Those tracks were never laid out for them and now the path of attachment was overgrown and formidable.

We took a lunch break at a gas station. Reagan picked at meals and Andrey ate enough food to sink a freightliner. We passed field upon golden field of sunflowers on the two-hour drive back to Sofia, and that is how long our beautiful, brief honeymoon lasted.

```
August 17, 2012
```

We are up and at 'em after a night with what felt like newborn twins. I don't think Reagan has slept at all, though she hasn't cried, either. I think they like us but they aren't sure what to make of these strange grownups. What's the Bulgarian word for "snuggle?"

August 18, 2012

Just checked the temperature for Sofia online. I was surprised when it said only 16 degrees Celsius, but then realized it's not even ten o'clock yet and it's supposed to get to 35 degrees Celsius later today. Converted to Fahrenheit, that's five degrees south of the temperature needed for baking pizza.

Wait, let me go just a little farther back. In the two years leading up to bringing Andrey and Reagan home, we completed all the paperwork and training required of adoptive families. And in the months and weeks prior to making that final pick-up trip, we had also made all the other preparations we could think of, including:

- Ordering a CD of common Bulgarian phrases. There was actually a track on it called "Nagging Parental," so I learned how to boss children bilingually (*Slez doly!* Get down! *Vnimavai!* Be careful!) and our kids discovered that the Bulgarian word for brother is "*brat*," which, as you can imagine, was met with a variety of reactions from the Guerralings.

- Organizing and rearranging almost the entire house. What worked in my head was very different from what actually worked when a tape measure was involved.

- Painting both kids' rooms: The girls got light pink. The boys got something deceptively labeled "South Pacific Blue," but upon application it turned about more like "Southcentral Alaskan Smurf."

In all the chaos of planning an overseas trip and preparing to bring home two children, I realized I forgot to put something crucial on our to-do list (which looked like *laundry vacuum package orders ship orders finish packing call the bank remember to breathe call the doctor take kids to the park don't forget to breathe clean the bathrooms take a shower put the kids to bed and FLY ACROSS THE WORLD)* but I fixed it in time, and *paint toenails* was put in its proper place near the top of the agenda. This was only right after the other imperative item we'd forgotten, which was to find someone to drive us to the airport.

But did we prepare for any of the emotional stuff? Not really. I mean, I think we felt like the two years of required trainings, readings, and meetings had covered all of that because it was all deeply emotional and pretty invasive, involving intense discussion, introspection, and evaluation.

So that first week in the hotel, we started to learn that *"...all that preparation was like going through earthquake survival drills – how to do first aid, how to take cover, how to evacuate safely – versus actually living through an 8-point earthquake. It was like the difference between learning CPR versus actually having to administer it to someone who has no pulse."* [1] That week we felt the first small tremors our adopted kids were going through: They both sucked their thumbs to self soothe. One flailed, rocked, and moaned in sleep, while the other either raged and screamed until the wee hours, or didn't sleep at all.

The artificial hothouse of a 95-degree hotel room without siblings, housework, or normal routines was an odd way to transition into life together. We saw the first glimpses of food issues with both overeating and under-eating, and we realized Reagan was used to mostly mushy food, with bibs. She flinched whenever I reached toward her to wipe her face or brush aside her hair, and often she threw her arm over her head to protect herself. The staff at her orphanage had said she was afraid of men, but she was fine around Vince; it was women she was terrified of.

She was also scared of using the toilet, and we quickly gave up on washing her underwear in the hotel bathroom and reverted to pull-ups. She initiated nothing for herself – no conversation, no play, no self-care, very little movement. If she needed to get onto an adult-sized chair, she could not climb and had to be lifted. She could not peel a banana. She expected everything to be done for her or to her.

The staff at her orphanage claimed she slept well, would eat anything, and was potty trained. Also came with a free unicorn.

But she was beautiful. Everyone noticed, and back in March when we met her, the orphanage staff implied that that must be why we chose to adopt her. As we walked through the city or went to appointments, various strangers, hotel staff, and even our attorney's assistants would touch her, pick her up, try to give her kisses, give her things without asking us, or coo at her in Bulgarian, and we had no idea what they were saying to her.

One night in the hotel restaurant, Reagan kept repeating something we couldn't figure out. Suddenly the server arrived with a plate piled high with cheese and put it in front of her.

"What's this for?" we asked. "We didn't order it."

"The little girl," he said, pointing at her and smiling. "She kept saying she wants cheese. So here you go."

"Um, thanks," we answered, "but she can't have that. Please don't give her something without asking us first." We had enough potty issues to navigate without adding "constipation until October" to the list. We moved the plate away, Reagan immediately threw a fit, and the server gave us a disapproving look. *Rude Americans.*

Lopsided kindness met irreconcilable cultural differences. We couldn't possibly know all the conventional expectations in this country, but we also couldn't sacrifice our own needs as a family to play nicey-nice with people who didn't understand what was happening, no matter how well meaning they were. We may have come off as rude, but it felt disrespectful to *us* as parents. More importantly, it was confusing to a child who had only known temporary adults in her life and it harmed the attachment process. *Strangers are nice, parents are mean.* Terrible message.

We learned to preface our requests for help with clarity and boundaries. And we started to realize that clarity and boundaries were to become a larger part of our lives than we ever imagined.

Our folded cheat sheet from the Bulgarian language CD started falling apart from constant use. We asked our kids if they were tired, hungry, thirsty, done, too hot, too cold, hurt, or if they needed to go to the bathroom. And in turn, we taught them important English words, too, like shoes, potty, sleep, and, uh, French fries.

We were honored to introduce them to so many things. Their new normal included lots of music, hugs and kisses, and prayer before meals. We read stories and drew pictures. We flew paper airplanes, rearranged the hotel room furniture, and made forts out of the couch cushions. We prayed again at bedtime and tucked them in, and learned that little boys everywhere have one thing in common, regardless of nationality, skin color, or up-bringing: When they fart, they giggle.

Mostly though, we walked every day. Miles and miles. Navigating the broken pavement and cobblestones of their homeland was great physical therapy for little legs that hadn't seen enough play – particularly for Reagan, who's jerking, awkward step was uncertain over every new surface. We visited all of the sights in Sofia we had seen in the spring, but this time we did it with the kids we went there for in the first place.

It wasn't the highlight of our sightseeing, but one of our required appointments was a trip to the U.S. Embassy for visas. Lots of rules there: No photos allowed, no cameras, no phones, no scissors, no suspicious movements, no swimming, no diving, no splashing. But I will always remember that Embassy with fondness because it taught me the value of air conditioning, which, as a lifelong Alaskan, had always been a vague enigma to me. Now I'm a believer.

We received two documents in Bulgarian, accompanied with English translations:

удостоверение за раждане

CERTIFICATE OF BIRTH

Our children's names were at the top of each one. Date of birth, place of birth. Under that, the word **майка**, mother. My full name, my date of birth. Under that, the word **баща,** father. Vince's full name, Vince's date of birth. Those documents are a perfect picture of what most people see on the surface of adoption: Legally, everything seems so cut and dried. Finished. *Ladies and gentlemen, we just rewrote history.* But there was (and is) no pretending that we are their birth parents. We *are* their parents now, and it's affirming to see that officially recognized, but it doesn't change the reality of their past.

We also received our court decree for the adoption. It was emailed to us before, but this was real paper, stamped, sealed, and signed. It said:

IN THE NAME OF THE PEOPLE, SOFIA CITY COURT, blah, blah, blah (skip three pages), DELIVERED THE FOLLOWING DECREE: **ADMITS FULL ADOPTION.**

A two-year process brought to fruition – on paper, at least.

That night was our last in Bulgaria, and we got Andrey's and Reagan's passports back, complete with their visas. The next morning a cab took us on the same drive that had introduced us to the country five months earlier, through slums with windowless buildings, laundry on clotheslines next to the road, and piles of rotting wood, decayed beyond recognition of their original purpose. Shiny cars parked by crumbling buildings and littered paths.

For the fourth and last time we walked the wide halls of the Sofia Airport, but this time for our return trip with Andrey and Reagan. Our feelings of exultation over bringing the fruits of our labor home were somewhat dampened by a constant struggle with one of our new darlings who wanted sole possession of our wheeled carry-on. He threw a fit in security lines, refused to go to the bathroom when opportunity arose, and then proceeded to writhe in agony while waiting in another line to check luggage.

Our trip home was only two flights – a short one with an overnight layover in Germany, and a long one right over the top of the Arctic Ocean back into Anchorage. Due to the time warp, we would arrive in Alaska twenty minutes before we left.

The pre-flight instructions on the first plane were all in Bulgarian, but I knew some of the language by then and I'm pretty sure the gist was, "In the unlikely event of an emergency, ask the six-year-old next to you for assistance since you have no clue what we're telling you to do." We took off, waved "ciao-ciao" to Sofia, and left an old homeland for a new one.

Similar to the dilemma of entertaining two kids in a hotel room, we faced hours on an airplane with even fewer options. Fortunately, Andrey was intrigued by the little packet of snack accoutrements that came with the sandwich dinner. Stir sticks were fascinating. Napkins, useful. Wet wipes, very handy in certain situations. But coffee creamer? That stuff was completely worthless until you finally managed to wrestle the packet open, in which case it made a wonderful mess and then you had something to do with the wet wipe.

We flew into Frankfurt. I had kicked and screamed against the idea of an overnight layover, thinking of dozens of what-if scenarios. Would another hotel further confuse Andrey and Reagan? What if they didn't sleep? What if we couldn't get a separate crib for Reagan? What if we took the wrong bus, lost our luggage, or got scammed at the hotel?

In the face of all these questions, we found our way to the shuttle terminal across the airport and suddenly I wasn't the only one kicking and screaming because at that moment we introduced Andrey and Reagan to their first experience with escalators. Fear and shrieking commenced in stereo accompanied by withering, judgmental looks from strangers who stared as we wrestled two violently resistant small children and all of our luggage down the moving staircase.

Once that was over, the layover in Frankfurt ended up being a gift. All my little reasons to panic were calmly met with God's peace and covering, and just like the escalator, it was meant to make our trip easier, even though I didn't see it that way at first. The hotel was close to the airport, the shuttle was swift and easy, and we were able to sleep for a solid eight hours before the ten-hour flight back to Alaska. Best of all, we had family stationed in Germany who arranged to stay at the same hotel for the night. We hugged, laughed, and introduced our kids, cousins who spoke different languages. It was our first sense of normalcy after weeks of foreign culture and struggling to communicate with Andrey and Reagan. We were still overseas, but our niece and nephews were American kids who did familiar American things, and we understood each other.

The next morning was the long flight home, filled with books, paper and crayons, a movie, an all-too-short nap, and lots of correction. We broke the monotony with field trips to the lavatory, where a sign was printed in large letters: "DO NOT FLUSH WHILE SEATED ON THE TOILET." I can only imagine the lawsuits that necessitated such a warning. (At least the sign was in English.)

Nine and a half hours later, we flew over the Mat-Su Valley. Over our home. And then across Cook Inlet. We touched down in Anchorage, and Andrey and Reagan became citizens of the United States of America.

We were the last ones off the plane, and it took an hour to wait in line and complete immigration paperwork. By the time we found our luggage piled in an abandoned bay all the other passengers were gone, but a few airport employees stood at a podium in the otherwise deserted area. They looked at us – exhausted, giddy, travel-worn, and almost home – and they knew who we were.

"There's a whole crew of people waiting for you guys," they smiled. "Right through there."

We pushed the double doors open and dozens of our people were on the other side. Our closest, best friends: The ones who had taken care of our kids. The ones who sold us the nine-passenger Suburban we named the Stagecoach. The ones who walked with us the whole way. And also Vincent, Ireland, Afton, and Chamberlain. They had been waiting for hours.

Someone took our first family photo -- all eight of us, photobombed by a taxidermied polar bear.

We filled every seat in the Stagecoach for the beautiful drive home. Then the real journey started.

2: to see the forest through the trees

And now we're caught up to where we started, as far outside the comfort zone as we could go. This was our second week all together, cocooning, which means we were hunkered down hermit-style in a loud kind of quiet with no visits, few outings, and much turmoil. Outside, it was still raining and we watched the water level closely as the ditch overflowed into our front yard; a flash flood nearby had already necessitated a rescue of ten people by raft.

We harvested our herbs and discovered that we had been saying "oregano" pretty often without realizing it. It was like this: Reagan would do any number of things, like knock over a project someone was working on, or turn the bathroom into a water park, or walk through someone's block construction, and the unvarying exclamation was, "Oh, Reagan, *noooo*!" (I confess that probably wasn't the exact phrase that came out of my mouth a couple times.)

Inside, we were already flooding – constantly on high alert, desperate for normalcy, dealing with more bodily fluids than you want to hear about, and doing it all on only four hours of sleep. You might already know that the rule of thumb for getting over jet lag is about one day of recovery for every hour of time difference from where you traveled, and you might also know – if you're an Alaskan, or a Bulgarian, or just truly gifted at acquiring mostly useless trivia – that Bulgaria is eleven hours ahead of Alaska. But there are a few other factors to consider. For example, if you travel with kids, you should add two days per child to that recovery. Subtract a day for every day's worth of pre-made meals waiting in your freezer. If you're female undergoing any kind of hormonal upheaval, like pregnancy, your monthly cycle, menopause, or a total absence of chocolate in your pantry, add another two days. Fortunately, you can shave two or three days off if you double or triple your caffeine intake accordingly.

But even still, you know it's survival mode when you're eating lunch three hours late and hear screaming upstairs, and you think to yourself, *Just one more bite, and then I'll go check.*

Our homegrown kids were at ease in Alaska's outdoors – in the woods, in the wonder, in the wild. Andrey and Reagan were uncertain about everything, because everything was new, including hikes, creeks, cats, and relatives. Somehow we needed to teach them that our home wasn't a different kind of orphanage, that Mom and Dad weren't just new staff, and that brothers and sisters weren't other kids in an institution. *Home* means comfort, warmth, and security; *family* means love and belonging. They didn't have any framework to hang those ideas on.

We knew it would take time. Because of the attachment issues involved, we knew we would be pretty much on our own. So we expected to be lonely for a while. We asked friends to pray over the state of our washing machine and espresso maker. But on the plus side, we remembered to keep used, caffeinated coffee grounds away from our curious new children who helped themselves to everything that looked remotely edible: crayons, erasers, kitchen sponges, compost.

"Eeshkam oshte!" they demanded. *I want more.* Even though they were both almost seven, Andrey and Reagan didn't even recognize the Bulgarian word for "please" and it was *eeshkam* everything in those first weeks: *I want a bath, breakfast, a snack, whatever you're holding, whatever that person is eating, and I want it now.* They didn't

know better, they weren't trying to be rude; it wasn't their fault that etiquette wasn't taught in orphanages full of dozens or hundreds of children.

Our first English lessons included learning *please, thank you,* and other magic words for routine manners. But no matter how we coached her, Reagan couldn't pronounce "be excused" at the table in her Bulgarian-English toddler speak. That was okay though, because a helpful sibling usually interpreted for her:

"Reagan wants to ride a caboose!"

"Reagan's asking to beat a caboose!"

"Mom, Reagan needs to be caboosed!"

It was a fight to teach every new, tiny thing to them, but after days of hypervigilance with two children whose needs threatened to flip everything in our home and lifestyle upside down, we clung to the old, healthy normal as much as we could. This is the way we do things: We read together, often. Kids ask to be excused when they're done eating. And we flush the potty, so help me – but only once, not eight times in a row.

In my journal, I wrote:

```
Reagan does toddler stuff all the time,
and now that we're learning her abilities
(or lack of them), we're finding our sense
of humor more often. But in the moment,
things are not funny. It wasn't funny when
I caught her washing a poopy Pull-up in the
toilet, because she's seen us do that with
her poopy underwear. It's not funny when
she falls down the stairs because she
either can't or won't balance without her
arms flapping wildly at her side. And it's
not funny when she's in the shower, facing
the spray, gasping and sputtering because
she won't turn around so the water is
against her back. She just doesn't know.
```

    And there is so much for us to learn
about what she does and doesn't know.

It was ten years before we learned Reagan's IQ, but we learned more about her challenges every week. Every moment felt burdened with more needs than could be possibly met, and the Lord told me this: *You only need to do what needs done in this moment. Not what needs done later today or tomorrow or next week, but just this very second. Not cleaning, not reading, not writing, not answering the phone or checking the mail. Just do what I am telling you* **right now.**

Often, He was telling me to sleep, or to go to the bathroom. By myself, even.

In the moments of frustration, anger, or fear, He said, *Just say My words. Listen to My songs. Tell them you love them...and just keep saying it.*

Piece by piece, they will learn. They have time. Peace by peace, you will learn. You have time, too.

On our third day of school as the parents of six kids, an empty bookshelf leaned back to dry out against a wall, its contents stacked in the hallway. Someone during morning chores had been highsticking with the broom and knocked over a vase, spilling water all over the top of the shelf and down the wall.

It was one of those easy messes to clean up, no big deal, only requiring you to move 250 pounds of books plus a large piece of furniture before you can wipe up all the water, which also entails discovering and cleaning four years' worth of saturated dust bunnies and grime hidden underneath, because I never rearrange furniture. Piece of cake. Nothing that two hours of sweat and labor couldn't fix.

But as I cleaned it, God told me He was scrubbing me, too. And each of us. It was a hard, craggy, boots-on-the-ground month of adjustment and we all needed His washing as the stress exposed muck that had needed washing for a long time – like colorful phrases that hadn't escaped in years, but came out when three of my fingertips were smashed by a smug, giggling girl who had been told over and over not to touch the kitchen drawers. I was brought facedown before a Father who needed to scrub me, and apparently it takes a lot of water to do this.

Other big interruptions scrubbed each of us. Little Reagan had fits before almost every meal because she smelled food cooking but couldn't eat it yet. They weren't tantrums, but more like the angry panic of a baby who didn't understand why the milk she craved had to be heated or cooled to the right temperature. I firmly cuddled her as she raged and eventually she calmed, and it occurred less and less over the following months. We showed her the process: runny cornbread batter that still needed to bake, and frozen containers of chili that needed to thaw and simmer. She watched the act of spreading peanut butter on bread, and learned that food is not instant.

I read *Johnny Tremain* to one of the kids that week, and came across this:

> *"Horses are timid animals at heart, but Goblin's the most timid of all."*
>
> *"Has he been treated badly?"*
>
> *"Yes – whipped because he's so timid. He had four owners in one year....He's not mean, nor a bully. He's as sweet and gentle an animal as you'll ever find. A piece of paper blowing in the street might make any horse shy – and he's ashamed of himself the next moment. But*

> *Goblin doesn't ever stop to see what it is. He thinks maybe it's a little white dog about to bite his heels and he jumps out of his skin....*
>
> *Sometimes it takes half an hour to quiet him again. As for clothes on the line, they aren't just shirts and petticoats. He thinks they are white hippogriffs big enough to carry horses off in their talons....*
>
> *"Now what you've got to do is get his confidence so completely he'll know you'll never let anything hurt him – you can't do that by whipping him.... Of course you'll be scared, but just remember this: no matter how scared you are, he's more so."*

- Esther Forbes, *Johnny Tremain*

Get their confidence so completely that they'll know you'll never let anything hurt them, it said.

Teach them the love that is deep and wide, God said, bursting at the seams and spilling everywhere, as the One who loves them scrubs their mama, too.

And mamas need a lot of scrubbing because we have days when a late lunch collides with helping a kindergartner with his handwriting, garnishing the tacos on our plates with eraser rubbings. We intercept crayons headed for the dryer but somehow cannot keep them from being thrown by little boys as missiles into their sibling's cup of tea. We have afternoons of waiting in line at the post office while being orbited by a toddler performing Ring Around the Rosie, make it to the counter during an encore presentation of If You're Happy and You Know It, and narrowly avoid the Hokey Pokey.

After a hard day of fighting children and fighting a cold, I flew to Psalms after tucking the kids in bed. My bookmark sat between chapters 56 and 57, both labeled in my Bible as "a miktam of David." It said, *Be gracious to me, O God, for man tramples on me, all day long an attacker oppresses me...*and I sank into the words:

> *They stir up strife, they lurk, they watch my steps*
> *as they have waited for my life.*
>
> *Be merciful to me, O God, be merciful to me,*
> *for in You my soul takes refuge;*
> *in the shadow of Your wings I will take refuge*
> *till the storms of destruction pass by.*
>
> *My soul is in the midst of lions,*
> *I lie down amid fiery beasts -*
> *the children of man whose teeth are spears and*
> *arrows, whose tongues are sharp swords.*
>
> *- Psalm 56:1, 6 and 57:1, 4*

And I thought, *Wow. "Miktam" must be Hebrew for "Parent's plea for divine mercy and rest from their kids."*

We ventured outside the walls of home a little at a time: to the doctor, to church, to the mountains at Hatcher Pass. We got gutsy and took all the kids in two carts out shopping. People delivered a few meals but we didn't have visitors. Piano lessons were on hold and so were dinners with friends.

The rain abated, the huge puddles receded, and in the mornings their surfaces were covered with sheets of ice that usually melted sometime during the day. The wind blew in the afternoon and leaves skidded across the yard. We started our third week of school, speaking mostly English and resorting to Bulgarian as often as necessary. But Afton was six and learning to read, and we discovered that he spoke Whale like Dory from *Finding Nemo*.

Let me illustrate:

Afton: "Buh...uUUh...nNn...buh...uuUnn...bunn..." (Insert inquisitive squinty look here.) "It sounds like *bun*?"

Me: There's no "n."

Afton, pointing to a letter: I was looking at the N.

Me: That's a T.

Afton: Oh.

He was saying sounds, but he was so caught up in the details that he missed the words they made. He missed the forest for the trees, and it was hilarious.

But I missed the forest for the trees, too, often. Almost daily, and it was not hilarious. I was caught up in the mess of diapers and laundry and attachment and squabbles, and outside the walls of our chaotic little haven were cancers and divorces and felonies, oh my, and the world was a hurting and hurtful place.

I journaled and blogged at night to document the days, but it quickly transitioned to prayer, processing, and the need to stay sane. I got sick of hearing the phrase "new normal," and both feared and resented that it meant the loss of wonderful, non-negotiable things from our old normal. Writing stopped the wind for a moment while debris settled everywhere, inside and out, and six little kids brushed their teeth and got ready for bed.

A reader emailed me that week, asking me to help clarify the great mission in motherhood for those of us who are in the thick of it – the never-ending laundry, dishes, discipline, teaching, and everything else – and I wrote back an unpolished confession of my own fogginess in that area. But after a few days of praying, some of my grasping and wandering started to come together and instead of speaking Whale, the words I was sounding out started to make sense.

For example, we each have a different mission in the details, but in the big picture we're called to the same things. We aren't all called to adopt, but we are all called to help the orphan. We aren't all called to be pastors, but we are all called to the Great Commission. We aren't all called to be in the military, law enforcement, or other public service, but we are all called to pray for our leaders and love our neighbor. These are all part of our mission.

Our mission is to bring light to dark places. Specifically for our family, part of our mission was declaring to the world that life is valuable; each child has a destiny that is not fulfilled in a neglectful institution, but in a family who will love and fight for them even if they fight against loving us back. Our mission was to change their future as we changed their diet, their focus, and the atmosphere they lived in. They're valuable enough to keep clean. They're worth teaching.

They have a great calling, and that calling begins with offering them a great childhood.

And that's an important distinction, because I had thought the mission was to *give* them a great childhood, including a great education. But now I know that giving also requires accepting and receiving, and those parts of the process are out of our hands. Even still, the Lord is teaching me which things are my responsibility and which ones are not. Offering is my responsibility. Choosing for others whether or not to accept and receive something is not.

Our mission is the big picture – that huge, glorious, messy forest made of all sorts of trees that seem to be in our way, and we often get lost in them. We work our tails off, sweat tears, and plow a trail that keeps growing over. The trees are in our way and going around them is time consuming and it all feels as effective as raking leaves in a windstorm.

This tree is in my way! That tree just scratched me! This tree fell down months ago and no one told me and it wasn't on the map and I just tripped over it! Will someone please get these trees out of here? **I'm trying to get to the forest,** *for crying out loud!*

Suddenly we realize, *Oh my goodness. The trees are... part of the forest.*

These mundane things get overlooked in the hope of raising our kids to be missionaries or surgeons or farmers or whatever, but what we are really doing in this season is laying a foundation for greatness. That foundation is built by doing laundry and reading books and teaching gentleness, good boundaries, and a million other things. The foundation is laid with humility and value for life. And as we build that foundation, we are strengthening our own.

That forest we are hacking our way through is there *because we have planted it.*

Where there was once an empty field, we brought life, gave birth, adopted into our family, and the trees started growing. The laundry pile got bigger. The dishwasher ran multiple times a day. The utilities got more expensive and the grocery bill kept spiking.

Our forest needs lots of cultivating. Yes, these things can be tedious and frustrating, but this is not the life of mediocrity. We clear the path and bleed life. This is the preparation for lives of greatness, and the mama who plants now is the mama who reaps glory later. This is the season of growth, for a great harvest.

So we eased into the school year with the basics, doing math and handwriting and other things at the table. Four kids crowded the dining room with school work and crafts, and two little girls sat on a blanket on the floor, sorting different colored buttons into a muffin tin. Chamberlain was three, and Reagan was undefinable.

People asked about her gross motor skills, fine motor skills, communication, potty training, self-control, cognitive ability...and we didn't have easy answers. She lived in an orphanage until she was almost seven, was the size of a four-year-old, and usually acted like a two-year-old. It took us weeks to begin to understand what we should really expect from her. Our doctor reassured us that her delays were probably entirely due to trauma and neglect (true), and declared they would be overcome as she was loved into our family (false). To be honest, none of it was comforting when we were on the fourth round of poopy underwear in 24 hours.

We didn't know yet that some things can't be healed by love. Our doctor, completely inexperienced with adoption, still had a lot to learn, too.

Now, as I sit here with you over this book with coffee in hand, I can tell you that "love heals all things" is a devastating half-truth. (And what are half-truths? Lies.) *God's* love heals all things, yes. But that's not what we mean by that. We usually mean *our* love heals all things, and our love is a whole different animal.

The danger is that we confuse love with affection. And when we need something or someone to be healed and people tell us "love heals all things," it is akin to saying that we aren't loving enough. Or we aren't loving the right way. Or maybe we aren't loving, period. We must not have this thing figured out, because if we did, it'd be fixed.

I thought, *If I could only drum up more warm fuzzies for these children who bristle at affection and return it with aggression, we'd have this in the bag.* So we, too, cried out *eeshkam oshte* because only the Savior's supernatural healing could fix this, and we were desperate for fixing. Only God can heal a brain so ravaged by exposure to alcohol in utero that the effects went all the way down to her toes.

> *One of the lies that the enemy beats us with is that there is something wrong with us if we're struggling to love our children. They're just little, we tell ourselves. Innocent. None of this was their fault. How can I dislike them so much?*
>
> *I'll tell you how: because trauma isn't very likable.*
>
> *That's right. It's not.*
>
> *HERE'S THE REALITY.*
>
> *A child who lies to you, spits at you, smears feces around your house, destroys things, attacks people, steals, urinates all over, sexually assaults others, sets up booby traps to harm others, keeps you awake with screaming or pounding, requires 24-hour supervision, or generally treats you like they'd sooner watch you die than spend time with you? Not very likable.*
>
> - Natasha Metzler [1]

What we eventually learn — usually through painful life experience — is that **love is obedience to God's calling**. It is not feelings of affection. Love does what is best for the beloved, usually at a cost to ourselves. Affection gets something in return, but love serves regardless of response or outcome.

It can take a long time to learn that the outcome isn't entirely up to us.

3: heavy wind

My first drive alone, away, alight, since coming home was a full month after the whirlwind at the airport. I was the crazy lady driving seventy miles an hour down the mountain, escaping on autopilot to a friend's house. I flipped turn signals instinctively, navigated the highway and neighborhoods without thinking, and found myself at her house thirty minutes later hardly knowing how I got there. And a few hours later when I got back home, I was happy – not realizing that when I left, I hadn't been.

```
October 29, 2012

Had a hard talk with a family member. It
was not a restful, Sabbath day activity,
but she called right after we got off the
phone with another difficult, nosy person,
so it looks like we weren't really destined
to observe the Sabbath this afternoon,
anyway.
Conversation is stilted so we walk on
eggshells. She has no idea what's going on
here, but she also has a hard time admit-
ting it. Or maybe she knows a little of
what's going on from reading our blog, but
won't admit that, either. My guess is the
latter, and she's curious.
She finally ventured to ask what's really
been weighing on her mind.
It's about Reagan.
```

"Is she..." Her voice dropped to almost a whisper. "*Handicapped*?!"

From many years of experience, I know she considers this the worst possible description of a person, so terrible that it's almost taboo.

And I thought, but did not say, "If you don't know by now, then it's none of your business."

One of our biggest challenges was the language barrier between us and our new kids. English is no peach to learn, but combined with attachment issues and manipulation it was impossible to tell – until it became obvious – that words were mispronounced on purpose and sentences were garbled intentionally. But it didn't help that our toddler tried to coach her new siblings in proper enunciation (Chamberlain to Andrey while I prepared dinner: "See dis? Dis is a *toe-tay-toe,* can you say toe-tay-toe? *Toetaytoe, Andrey*!") or that we watched movies with different accents and their quotes had become part of our daily conversation – like when the kids made a baptismal tank out of exercise mats and the first stuffed animal to get dunked was a shark puppet who, according to Afton, had come to know Jesus and was now "a nice shahk, an' not a fewoshus mahn-eating creechah."

I'm thinking none of this helped Andrey and Reagan learn American English.

But also, another big challenge was that most people still didn't understand what was going on and I couldn't keep track of who we'd explained certain things to.

We watched closely to see how Andrey and Reagan handled being around other people: how they interacted with them, how they approached them, and how they tried to get attention from them. We didn't allow them to hug other adults and we asked our friends to not pick them up, hold their hands, give them food, or have any other affectionate contact. It's a long road for a child who has never attached to anyone to learn that love, safety, and affection come from Mama and Daddy and not from every random adult they encounter. Babysitters and childcare were out for months to come. Banquets and fundraisers were also out, and weekly classes and small groups had to wait until next year.

Well-meaning loved ones told us how glad they were that we were home and finished with this process. They had the impression that adoption ends at the airport and everything afterward is rosy and enchanting.

But it's not over. And also, it's not like having a baby, or having twins, or adding two of your friends' kids to your family. It is like adding thirty kids to your family, and constantly trying to figure out which two are showing up at any given time. It is like feeding eight new kids. It is learning to give consistent love to someone who returns it with capricious regard and sometimes resists love altogether. It is the battle to protect everyone and still allow freedom to grow and move. It is a war zone, and some days it shows.

In the middle of the night, in the middle of a cold, I was awake and not breathing. I gave up tossing and turning, waiting for gravity to clear my sinuses, and got out of bed, found tissues, filled the humidifier, and went to the kitchen to grab a fresh glass of water.

On the way downstairs, something out the window caught my eye and stopped me. The sky was green, and moving. And God said, *Go to the window seat and sit down with Me. I want to talk to you.*

I briefly protested. *Don't You know it's 2:00 a.m. and I have six kids and I've been sick for five days?*

He said, *Yes. Go sit down and rest with Me. Catch your breath.*

So I sat down and rested. I looked out the window, watched the northern lights, and started to breathe again. He listened to me rattle on about all of the overwhelm, all the family stuff: internal uproar as we adjusted to our new family dynamics, and external heartache with parents divorcing and conflicts in ministry and friends facing crises. We'd had several life changing phone calls in the past few weeks.

I told Him, *Wave to me if You're still listening*, and the northern lights jumped in an arc of green fire. He was right there. He talked to me and there was peace inside. And I knew I was only getting a few hours of sleep, but a deeper kind of rest was happening and it healed me, too.

The Holy Spirit said, *That family member you love, who you thought felt badly toward you, who disparaged you? He doesn't feel badly toward you, he feels badly about himself. He needs your prayer desperately.*

He said, *That person who accused you? Give that to me. It's okay. You are not thinking too highly of yourself, You are thinking highly of Me. Someday she will understand that.*

He said, *Those days that feel messy and off-track, with cat puke and poopy diapers and broken dishes and temper tantrums? Those are days that remind you that you are in a war. You chose obedience over sterility. Wars are messy, and must only be entered into with a great mission in focus. Remember your great mission.*

After a while I went back to bed and woke up tired and tackled a new day anyway. There were so many messes and there was one day that week when Reagan broke three dishes before we got another one of those life changing phone calls.

> *By awesome deeds you answer us with righteousness, O God of our salvation, the hope of all the ends of the earth and of the farthest seas; the one who by his strength established the mountains, being girded with might; who stills the roaring of the seas, the roaring of their waves, the tumult of the peoples, so that those who dwell at the ends of the earth are in awe of Your signs.*
>
> *You make the going out of the morning and the evening to shout with joy.*
>
> *– Psalm 65:7-8*

God breathes on us to do things all the time – big things like adoption, small things like sitting down with Him at two in the morning. He tells us to do things that are understood by some and misunderstood by others. The civilian details are not so important, but if He tells you to do something, go. Sit down and talk to Him. He has incredible things to say. And if you ask Him to wave...I think He will.

Days of wind continued – incessantly, always on this mountain – and it was a beautiful, lovely, hateful thing. I loved watching the trees bow and the grasses fly and the leaves twirl up in little tornadoes. I loved it from this side of the window, with blankets, steaming tea, and the woodstove going full-bore. But on the other side of the window I've never been real fond of the wind. I can't breathe in it; it's dirty and makes my hair feel gross.

I used to love listening to the wind howl at night until one storm felled a birch tree on our roof and I realized how dangerous the wind could be. Suddenly, listening to the raging noise lost its romantic charm. The volume came in waves, and from under the warmth of a down comforter I wondered if this gust or the next one was going to bring another tree down on us.

So I stayed awake, listening and wondering and praying while it roared, rattling the chimney, whistling across the stovepipes, occasionally shaking the walls. Gusts up to eighty miles an hour are considered hurricane force outside of Alaska, but here they're just "heavy wind."

But that windstorm taught me to pursue peace. In the wild gusts, I knew I was still protected. I learned to declare and remind myself that I was still safe, and I reveled in knowing the danger of the wind while also knowing my own perfect security in the middle of it, because the One who keeps the winds is the same One who holds me. And on good days, the louder it got, the more I leaned into His peace.

```
November 1, 2012

Stealing time while the bigger kids are
outside playing in the wind, and Cham is in
her bed with another stomachache.
   I'm hurting, fighting depression, wanting
a mentor to talk to and confide in, and I
don't know who to talk to. When we've most
needed support and encouragement, we've
felt unwelcome, micromanaged, and ignored.
And who has time to listen to all of my
problems and wounds, anyway? I don't even
have time for them.
   In spite of the wind, the sun is shining
and I am so grateful. Hopelessness and de-
```

spair are a little more manageable with bright sunbeams in the house.

A week before she turned seven, we dedicated Reagan and Andrey at church. One of our pastors and friends read this over us:

> *Praise the Lord!*
> *Blessed is the man who fears the Lord, who greatly delights in his commandments! His offspring will be mighty in the land; the generation of the upright will be blessed.*
>
> *- Psalm 112:1-2*

But in my own heart, most days I did not delight in His commands. I didn't delight in being manipulated, I didn't delight in cleaning bodily fluids or life turning upside down. I didn't delight in the assumptions of others, or hearing their judgments passed along in a grapevine manner, or in the ignorant advice of those who knew nothing about adoption or attachment issues and had no interest in learning.

And even though we were there faithfully every Sunday, I definitely did not delight in church anymore, which astonished me. It had always been the highlight of my week; it was when I heard the Lord in new ways and learned new things from His word. It was when I saw friends, and actually did my hair, and had conversations with other adults. But now on Sundays we were constantly on high alert, hypervigilant over boundaries with adults who often unwittingly responded to our kids in ways that inflamed them the most.

I didn't know then that church is often the hardest place for newly adoptive and special needs families. I just thought we were failing. I thought we were alone. Neither were true, but all the evidence pointed that way and I didn't know better.

I also didn't know until later that we were in the middle of a complex, coordinated spiritual attack that had been in the works for months, timed precisely to hit when we were the most vulnerable. Now I can look back and tick off the aggregate of events that had nothing to do with our adoption but still accumulated pain in that season: a family member dying of cancer, another going to prison, and another we needed to entirely sever all contact with. One set of our parents announced their divorce. Our closest friends were moving thousands of miles away. And there was also a ministry situation that occurred right before we left the country to bring Andrey and Reagan home; it was still not resolved and completely out of our hands.

A ministry leader had invited me out for coffee – a social meeting, she'd said, just to catch up before our lives changed and we would be off the radar for a while to adjust with our new children. We chatted for two hours and then I needed to go to a legal appointment to update documents before going overseas.

Wait a minute, she said, and pulled out a paper. I took it and recognized excerpts of a homeschooling post I had written on my personal blog. The meeting's true agenda was revealed as she proceeded to unload a reel of indignations she had felt upon reading it, saying I had misrepresented the church and the ministry I served in. She said the pastoral leadership was frustrated and disappointed with me, and had asked her to speak to me about it.

Not everyone had the privileges I had as a married woman, she castigated, recounting when she was a single mom and made choices that were different from those I had made with my own life and my own kids.

And that, at least, clarified things a little: This was personal, about her own offense. That was obvious, and I could tell that what she had said was not the whole story. But my face was warm and my heart beat loudly; I was stunned that the meeting had taken this turn and I tried not to cry in the middle of the busy cafe. There was no time to process it and I was late for my next meeting, and the few words of defense I mustered were interrupted and cast aside. I was horrified to think that I had grieved our pastoral staff, but I was equally horrified at the prospect of our church leadership presuming my personal blog was their property for public relations, requiring pastoral sanction and approval.

The whole time we were in Eastern Europe, this was on my mind as I documented our days on my website and felt unknown critics looking over my shoulder. *Are you sure it's okay to write that?* the accuser hissed. *What if so-and-so thinks you're implying such-and-such?*

Six weeks after coming home, we asked to be put back on the rotation for serving in ministry, desperately needing a semblance of normalcy wherever we could find it. But we were denied by the same ministry leader, citing "our issues hadn't been resolved yet" – and that was interesting, because her accusations were against me, but Vince wasn't allowed to serve yet, either. (He was, after all, the husband who, um, gave me privileges). The lead pastor was in and out, traveling the country, and there was no way to resolve the issue until we could schedule a meeting together. *When can we do that?* I asked. *Probably not for months,* they said.

It was February, six months later, when I finally sat down with the lead pastor and he apologized, explaining what that initial meeting had been supposed to convey.

And it was years before a few other leaders elucidated the full story of how things had been misrepresented.

But at the time, I had promised not to talk to anyone else in church about it to avoid causing division, which left me with no one to process it with. Every Sunday for six months I felt not only the judgment toward my family over our kids' behaviors along with the frustration of explaining attachment boundaries to people who didn't understand them, but I was also haunted by the insecurity of wondering which pastors and leaders were so upset with me. I felt resented and unwelcome, and it overshadowed our first several months as adoptive parents, deepening the isolation we lived in. Even though the ministry debacle had nothing directly to do with our adoptions, in the spiritual realm the timing had everything to do with it.

So instead of fearing the Lord, I feared I was failing. I feared for the future, and the changes in our immediate and extended family. I feared what other people thought of us, and I hated that I cared about it. Heedless, hurtful words were like wind on smoldering tinder, and my spirit started to burn in the worst ways.

4: fighting phantoms

Probably every family with small children goes through a season of ailments appearing out of nowhere at bedtime: There's A Fuzzle In My Eye, My Throat Is Sore Even Though I've Been Playing Happily All Day, or I Left My Water Bottle Downstairs And I'm ReallyReallyReallyReally Thirsty. Or, the slightly more ambitious I Lost My Favorite Stuffed Animal And I Think He's in the Car So Can I Please Go Get Him?

Afton's most recurrent ailment was the one called I Have A Tummy Ache. Unlike Chamberlain's stomachaches that put her out of commission for hours (we eventually realized they were dairy related), his were more comical and like clockwork.

I offered him some apple cider vinegar diluted with water – which, if you've never tried it, truly *is* a good remedy for a tummy ache – and he hesitantly agreed, but asked me to add honey to it.

"Nope, no honey after bedtime," I said, glancing over at Andrey, who was watching carefully. I could tell he was seriously considering whether or not he wanted a tummy ache, too. "Still want some though, with no honey?"

Afton put on his most feeble voice and weakly whimpered assent. A few minutes later, I was back upstairs with a tiny cup of what I hoped would fix this for at least a few weeks. It should be noted that these children were healthy all day and had no signs of a fever, illness, or any other decrepitude besides not wanting to submit to bedtime.

I handed it to him and snuck another look at Andrey, who was sneaking a look at Afton while holding his tummy and letting out the faintest moan. Afton held the cup, and Andrey experimented with a louder whimper and looked at me. Poor kid had no idea yet what apple cider vinegar was, so I grinned and told him to watch his brother.

Afton took a drink, swallowed, made a face, shuddered, and handed the cup back, and... ladies and gentlemen, it was a miracle. Turns out, apple cider vinegar is so corrective for tummy aches that you don't even have to be the one who drinks it to be cured.

The days and nights ran together, full and exhausting. A friend asked how long we'd been home, and I counted the months off.

"September, October, January...three months," I said.


```
November 21, 2012

    It's Reagan's birthday. She refused to
eat and fussed and cried through her first
meal of the day. At lunch I disguised her
rejected leftovers as soup, which usually
works, but not this time. Everyone else was
outside playing while she still sat there,
vacantly stirring her soup, watching her
siblings through the window and giggling at
them.
My back was to her while I scrolled on
the computer. It is her birthday, and to-
morrow is Thanksgiving, and I feel no joy
for either event. I still can't wrap my
mind around her and Andrey actually being
home and being ours - it feels like pre-
tend, it feels like a loan, sometimes it
feels like a nightmare - and I fear I am
losing this time that should be cherished.
But I don't understand it at all; I'm bare-
```

ly staying above the surface between gulping, choking mouthfuls of salt water.

It is her birthday and I'm feeling guilty. Always feeling guilty. I scrolled through photos of our friends who are touring Jerusalem where Jesus walked, and was acutely aware that my back was turned on my daughter during her birthday lunch, while she refused another meal and missed out on playtime outside. And I tried to ignore the guilt, so I looked more closely at a photo of a rock in Jerusalem that Jesus is said to have stood on and taught from.

And I thought, Wow. You were there. Right there.

And He said, *I'm right behind you. Right here.*

And I know He is. He's the One who sat with her in the chair, and He's also the One sitting with me in my grief and grappling.

So I turned around and sat with her, and Him. She finally drank the broth, until just the itty bitty chunks of meat were left. I took her spoon and found the smallest of small pieces, and scooped it up.

"Soup?" She opened up, took a bite. And another, and another. She let me feed her, and eventually finished the last of it on her own.

People keep telling me I need to write a book on our adoption experience. I'm usually so miserable I can't see how it would inspire anyone.

But if I ever do write a book, I will be sure to include this snappy bit of counsel:

A child who will use an entire roll of toilet paper in one trip to the bathroom is probably also a child who cannot be trusted with a small ration of toilet paper, since

```
they will just use the shower curtain to
wipe with instead.
```

After three months of being her mother, I discovered that Reagan could put pajamas on by herself. Everyone else already knew that, though.

Whenever I was with her at bedtime she whimpered in helplessness over putting on her zippered footie pajamas. Finally, someone – Vince, or maybe Ireland – informed me that they'd seen her do it by herself repeatedly. *What*? I was stunned, and asked around, and yep, everyone else knew she could do it. But she wanted help from me, so she feigned inability. Which, on one hand, was good: She actually wanted nurturing. But also, not good: She'd been deceptive about it, and somehow I'd been fooled for months.

Other secret superpowers we discovered included her ability to put on her own shirts, and Andrey's capacity to zip his own zippers (plus a talent for working the baby proof locks on doorknobs and cabinets). Helplessness and tantrums ensued every time we caught on and enforced independence.

Everything took so much time, there wasn't any left over for interruptions. We screened phone calls, ignored solicitors, missed meetings, and made a lot of extremely stupid-simple meals. That first winter, putting on snowpants took Reagan at least an hour – partly because of developing motor skills, and partly because of unsuccessful pleading for other people to do it for her. By the time she was dressed, everyone else was done sledding and coming back inside.

One afternoon was spent waiting for her to cooperate with changing a stinky diaper. I would not force her or wrestle her and she sat in the mess, jerking and fretting and protesting, unwilling to be changed. What makes someone want to sit in...that...for so long, when someone loves you and wants to help you get cleaned up?

> *How do I tell a child I love her when she doesn't know love? How do I expect her to trust me when all she has ever known is broken trust? I prove it. I earn it...When a child bites me, hits me, or looks into my eyes and tries to shove me away so she can hurt me before I hurt her, when a child overeats to the point of vomiting because she was once so hungry and is afraid of that hunger or she hides food under her covers "just in case"...what then?*
>
> *I love anyway. I get on my knees and I cry to God about the hurt they have experienced and I ask Him why. And then I remember that a good God who wants good for His children can only give good. I remember that all of this, even this hard part, is working for the good in their lives, for the good of God and His kingdom. I remember that these hardships are gifts that He is using to strengthen us as a family and in Him so that He may transform us into His likeness.*

- Katie Davis [1]

The temperature dropped to minus ten in December. This was not the best time for our washer to break, but there it was: Vin fixed it three times for three different issues, and though he finally got it to wash, spin, and rinse, it rattled the house in protest. But the noise diminished if you put at least one kid on top of it – the washer, not the house, I mean.

We put up the Christmas tree and saved all the breakable ornaments until after the probationary period was over, which we hoped would be sometime before January. The kids had free reign with all the other ornaments, hanging them in clusters off the same five branches while completely neglecting the rest of the tree. And for the first time ever, I didn't bother rearranging them.

We had lights and greenery, candles out of reach, and paper snowflakes all over the ceiling. I was enchanted enough to ignore the wonky tree and almost forgot about what had been wiped on our shower curtains.

This was the season that taught me there are only so many things I have a say over. For example, I could decorate the inside of the house, but I had no say over the temperature outside. I couldn't manage the weather, but I could manage the thermostat. I could provide clothes for the girls, but I could not keep them from dressing up as Rainbow Brite, Punky Brewster, or Gooney Bird Greene. I could make all kinds of snacks and dinners and treats, but I could not, not, *not* make a child eat certain foods. You can lead a boy to celery, but you can't make him eat it.

Outside our home, I couldn't heal marriages or fix bodies or detox addicts. Inside our home, it wasn't always twinkle lights and hot tea. I couldn't force obedience or manipulate learning any more than Reagan could negotiate the relationship between a turtleneck and a plastic clothes hanger. (But she *was* learning motor skills and English simultaneously. As she put her shirt on one morning, she poked herself in the eye, screamed, and then yelled, "I'm! *Sorry!*" to herself.)

Andrey and Reagan finally experienced their first Christmas with a family and everything was new: *Why is there a tree in the house? Why are there little lights everywhere?* They didn't know who Santa was, and as far as we could tell, they'd never had any kind of Christmas before.

We all have our own odd traditions. In our family, in lieu of the ever-popular new underwear in stockings, we have boxes of tea and treats like peppered cashews and dried fruit. That Christmas, our three smallest ones each got their own tea mug. And Reagan got her own hairbrush, making her immediately suspicious of a holiday in which people give each other instruments of torture.

We had no big traditional meal on Christmas Eve or Christmas Day that year. We saw family both days, but we also missed other family events on both days. Christmas wasn't the same and it would never be the same; our family had changed. Our extended family was changing. And it was not normal.

It wasn't so bad for us, though. We had loved ones who were starting completely over, who spent Christmas in the hospital, or who were without a home entirely. That Christmas, that year, those places weren't normal, either.

We tend to think life should be like a nice Christmas photo: quirky enough to be charming, but please, none of that messy reality that shows infection and pain underneath needing intervention. But life happens and sometimes we don't have a choice between unconventional or inconvenient or heartbreaking.

Jesus was here in the midst of it, and the holiday is made for those of us who live in the messy places. He was born in a barnyard shelter, delivered by an unmarried teenager on a dirt floor, with a carpenter for a midwife. His first bed was a feeding trough. He was adopted by a man who was not His biological father. He intimately knows the awkward and heartbreaking – He was gossiped about His entire life, and finally sentenced to death on trumped-up charges by people unworthy to walk in His shadow.

But He rose again, three days later. He walked out of that cave alive.

Life is irregular and excruciating and bizarre, but He wrote the book on unconventional living. In whatever kind of not-normal we are in, in all of the pain and strangeness and unknown, He is Emmanuel: God with us. There's nowhere we can go, or be taken, or suddenly find ourselves in, where He will not meet us.

When it all feels bleak and we have no idea what will happen tomorrow, He's with us, making us like Him. Walking with us, making us uncommon. And He will lead us out of the cave alive, too.

My big milestone before the end of the year was going on an outing with all six children by myself. I know it sounds so minor, but I dreaded errands even before we adopted. I hate shopping, small talk, introducing myself to strangers, waiting in lines, driving in the snow, looking around for the right kind of cheese, piling kids into and out of grocery carts, and fumbling for the right card in my wallet to pay with. (Grocery stores will *not* take library cards, even if you don't have any current fines.)

But this was the smallest of small outings. We got in the Stagecoach, picked up a parcel – the kids didn't even get out of the car – and we came back home. Still, it took almost an hour from the time I said "Shoes and coats!" to the time we pulled back into the garage and took them off again.

It was a beautiful drive, though. Clear and windy, snowdrifts everywhere. Flurries swirled across the road like an outbreak of snowy tornadoes, and during exceptional gusts, snow swept like a huge white phantom from one side of the road to the other. That's all it was, though, a phantom.

We got caught behind a school bus and I considered taking a detour to avoid all the stops. I thought again though, and followed it, praying for the kids as they got off the bus and made their way home. It was 3:00 p.m. and the sun was already setting.

Back home while getting dinner ready, Reagan melted down. She refused to get out of the kitchen, get out of the way, get out of the fridge, or get out of my face while I was trying to chop veggies and make sandwiches. That sounds harsh but it's not safe for kids to wedge their way between mama and the food cooking on the stove. She went stiff and wouldn't leave the kitchen, and we moved immediately into holding while Vincent finished making dinner for me.

She wasn't starving. She'd gained a lot of weight and a couple of inches of height already since August. But I think she was afraid that maybe she would be left out, maybe food wouldn't come, maybe it was only there to tease her. She drove through phantoms, too.

At church the previous Sunday it was ten below zero when we walked up the steps from the parking lot. Reagan was (and still is) a slow stair climber and she used to cling to railings for dear life, like a person who doesn't swim clings to the edge of a pool.

That morning, the metal railing was so cold that it hurt to touch it, but she wouldn't let go even as she shrieked from the pain. She refused to hold our hands and she refused to move, and just stood there crying as people walked around us.

Awkward seconds ticked by while we froze and waited, the air thickening around all eight of us from the fog of our breathing. I thought, *Surely she won't leave her hand there*...but she did. Ten below is common in Alaska, but hypothermia and frostbite aren't things to mess with so I removed her hand and picked her up; she stiffened and wailed in protest the entire way up the stairs until I put her down at the top of them.

Sometimes I wondered if people looked at us and thought, *Wow, what's the big deal about taking six kids out? What's her problem?* I wondered if they noticed a certain child still in oversized diapers and thought we were bad parents. I wondered if people thought I was nuts when they gushed over Andrey and tried to hug him or ruffle his hair, and the Mama Bear in me came out and said, "Thanks so much, but *please don't touch him*." Maybe they thought he had something contagious. Maybe they thought I was strangely controlling. Honestly, I *felt* strangely controlling. But those well-meaning people had no idea how their affection created turmoil in his heart, and how that turmoil manifested as devastating behaviors that created more trauma in our house.

So I fought phantoms, too.

When our posse walked through church or the store or the library, I hoped people didn't always feel like they had to take a detour to avoid all of our stops. I hope they prayed for us while waiting, while we made our way home.

5: let it break

This is a good time to confess that I kept forgetting I had six kids now.

I don't mean that I forgot *about* the kids, which was impossible with the amount of noise they made; I constantly counted "onetwothreefourfivesix" just to make sure I knew where everyone was. What I mean is that I kept forgetting – or just had not really grasped yet – that I was a mother of six kids. Mine, for keeps. I could hardly keep track of the days, and no matter how fast we went, there was never enough time to clean everything, read everything, learn everything, teach everything, cook everything, and still make sure everyone's toenails were clipped. It was a season of running, and as much as I love slow, simple living, it was no longer possible.

I couldn't simultaneously do laundry, break up an argument, supervise chores, keep dinner from burning, or answer the phone while holding a raging child, and I vividly remember lecturing Vincent and Afton one night that, no, this was *not* a good time to teach Andrey about spit wads. I was in the middle of yelling at them to put away the straws before I discovered the paper they were using included several business receipts.

But those big kids, only six, nine, and twelve at the time, were also the ones who came to the rescue, turning off burners, reading to little ones, wiping up messes, and making scrambled eggs in a pinch when my hands were full.

We had an unofficial buddy system: the kids were all buddies with each other, and I was buddies with Sophie, my thirteen-year-old cat. When I needed a break I sometimes escaped to my room for a few minutes and she was usually curled up on the bed – a great listener, rarely made messes, and never complained about the food. Plus, she could handle her own conflicts.

We multitasked and let go of non-essentials, and still, life was a blur. I cleaned accidents in the bathroom and refereed children and checked the hard-boiling eggs on the stove and realized I left my cup of tea somewhere upstairs, and found myself burping a swaddled stuffed animal that Chamberlain left in my custody.

I ran into Proverbs after plowing through Psalms, and chapter four, verse twelve caught my eye. When I read it, I collapsed as one who finds an unexpected timeout during an offensive push.

> *When you walk, your step will not be hampered, and **if you run,** you will not stumble.*

Oh my word. Tell me again!

If I run, I won't stumble? You mean...it's really okay to feel like life is at full tilt and zooming by? It's okay if there are seasons that are just like that? Because part of life *is* walking, but if you run because you have to and it still feels like things are being left undone, untouched, and unheeded, and slowing down means giving up, falling down, and crashing, it's okay to just *run*.

Amid all the well-meaning messages on social media and in books and in women's Bible studies about slowing down – and I am all for those messages – I found amazing sanction in that verse about running.

Sometimes we have to run to be healed; sometimes a marriage, a child, or a life is at stake. Sometimes we have to run just because dinner must be made so children can be fed and work can be done and mommy can get to bed by midnight. God knows, and it's okay. He is our rest in the running, and the spotter who keeps us from stumbling.

January 21, 2013

Stealing time to write while sitting on the closed toilet, scribbling frantically while coaching our preschooler through the motions of taking a shower and washing her hair, which she insisted she could do by herself.

"Are you sure?" I ask.

"Yes...*Waaaahhh*!!" comes the answer as shampoo goes in all the wrong places.

My schedule book collects miscellaneous scraps of thoughts and observations everyday, but that's no way to organize writing material into coherent memories. For example, Reagan is speaking more and more, though it's Bulgarian toddler babble instead of English, and usually impossible to decipher. She reverted back to saying "*Da me!*" (Gimme!) but can also demand food in English with perfect enunciation and obnoxious repetition.

Our contact teacher met them today. She, like so many others, was impressed with how calm Reagan was in public. But everyone is impressed with her when she's sitting at church, at a meal, whatever, because she's so content to just sit and not do anything. People think it's great behavior (and yes, the calm is better than a public tantrum any day of the week) but this is part of why she's so delayed – she's content to do nothing for hours on end. No initiative, no

```
acting on curiosity. It's not a reflection
of great behavior, but of profound neglect.
   Our current focus among a multiplicity of
other little things is getting her in and
out of the Stagecoach without needing to
lift her in and out like a baby. Her feet
are still nervous on ice, snow, and every
patch of unfamiliar ground.
```

I want to sit down with you over a huge mug of tea and tell you how, in spite of the turmoil (and thanks to homeschooling six kids), that was the season I discovered books by Elizabeth Goudge and Elizabeth Enright and Charles Kingsley. And I finally, *finally*, after many years, finished reading all of Jane Austen's published works, though there are only seven of them and I hid behind a locked bathroom door more than once to make it happen.

But instead, I have to tell you about Saturdays. The nerdy amongst us will talk about books and tea later.

Saturdays in those years were Fridays for us, and I used to dread them. Well, *dread* is a strong word, but let's say...nope, "dread" is right on target. It wasn't because the weekend was finally almost here, but because it was the only day I had to get up early and we spent it doing chores, finishing school for the week, and getting ready for the weekend.

After a particularly terrible night, Vin asked me in the early morning, "Are you listening to His music, and saying His words?" He knew what God had been speaking to me about, but he also knew I needed reminding. So on Saturdays I put worship music on to help move us through the day. We steeped in it until the atmosphere changed, and regardless of what was happening in the moment, it helped maintain our joy. Usually.

On one of those Saturdays while the bigger boys were upstairs doing impertinent things with a vacuum cleaner, I was downstairs holding the littler boy, who was raging in my arms. Two little girls danced around us to the music.

He was actually upset *because* the music was playing, and had demanded we turn it off. He tried to shut his door so he (and his brothers) couldn't hear it, but what he was really doing was hiding behind a hardened shell that had been cracking ever since we brought him home. He usually loved music, often asked for it, but he fought it this time out of opposition. He didn't realize he was trying to reject us and protect himself from healing. He was an unborn baby in the warmth of the amniotic sac, not wanting to come out into the light. But the waters broke, and he'd been screaming ever since he had his first breath of air.

We listened to the music anyway. We read books anyway. We hugged and loved anyway, and Jesus was, and is, the remedy. I'm convinced that The David Crowder Band and *The Chronicles of Narnia* were made for such a time as this.

> *"Are you not thirsty?" said the Lion.*
>
> *"I'm dying of thirst," said Jill.*
>
> *"Then drink," said the Lion.*
>
> *"May I – could I – would you mind going away while I do?" said Jill.*
>
> *The Lion answered this only by a look and a very low growl. And as Jill gazed at its motionless bulk, she realized that she might as well have asked the whole mountain to move aside for her convenience.*

> *The delicious rippling noise of the stream was driving her nearly frantic.*
>
> *"Will you promise not to – do anything to me, if I do come?" said Jill.*
>
> *"I can make no promise," said the Lion.* [1]

Another Saturday, we were finishing cocoa after playing in the snow. Dishes were in the sink waiting to be washed, and Andrey pointed to a particularly nasty pan.

"May pees crub dat?" he asked. He loved scrubbing dishes, and I loved that about him. But eggs were encrusted in it from breakfast. I ran the water and explained that he had to wait until it soaked for a while, because when we soak first, the scrubbing is easier. He agreed to wait a little while and went off to play.

Then Reagan brought her cup into the kitchen and it had been *so long* – almost two weeks? – since she had broken a dish, but I heard this one shatter as she walked to the counter. Glass in a million pieces, everywhere, and she was stepping in it while I ran to her.

She wasn't startled by the cup breaking; she was startled when I lifted her out of the glass, ripped off her sock covered in shards, and threw it in the burn bin. She bore down and tried to fight me while I checked her feet, which were fine, but glass was everywhere and she wouldn't stay out of the kitchen while I cleaned up the mess. Timeout followed, but she fought that also and tried to leave the room, to leave me.

She rejected us in defense to keep from being rejected first by us. But she didn't realize that, of course. It was like choosing life in a cage with no food and water while the door was wide open. She was like an abused woman who has been in a bad relationship for too long, but refused to break it off because freedom and healing are just too foreign and frightening.

> *"I daren't come to drink," said Jill.*
>
> *"Then you will die of thirst," said the Lion.*
>
> *"Oh dear!" said Jill, coming another step nearer. "I suppose I must go and look for another stream then."*
>
> *"There is no other stream," said the Lion.* [2]

I couldn't keep her safe in the kitchen, but I couldn't let her leave my sight either, so we moved right into holding. My cheek was against hers and she turned away. Her eyes went everywhere but to mine.
Jesus, I need Your words. He was right there and didn't make me wait for an answer.
"Let it break," I whispered to her.

> *It never occurred to Jill to disbelieve the Lion – no one who had seen his stern face could do that – and her mind suddenly made itself up. It was the worst thing she had ever had to do, but she went forward to the stream, knelt down, and began scooping up water in her hand. It was the coldest, most refreshing water she had ever tasted.*
>
> - C.S. Lewis [3]

"He has made you well," I whispered. And He has. She is a beautiful girl, crooked toes and all. No one misses her eyes when they first see her.

"He is making you well..." And He is. When we brought her out of the orphanage, she couldn't put on a jacket or recognize any letters, and she had parasites. Three hurdles overcome, a million to go.

We watched them resist the Lion at the stream of living water all the time. We steeped in His words, His music, and He was breaking up the nasty chaff that had encrusted them for almost seven years, and He was softening calcified areas in me that I didn't know existed. The hard scale of insecurity, fear, pride – they're all the same thing, really – build up for a long time. They only break off with His water.

```
February 27, 2013
```

Six months ago at this moment, I was unconscious from the stupor of jet lag. We flew the victory lap over Europe, over the Arctic Circle, and over the moon with our newly redeemed son and daughter.

I've been slowly coming to ever since. The fog is lifting and the sun is shining and I almost never feel like I just got whacked by the freezer door...except for the other day when I *did* get whacked by the freezer door...anyway, I usually feel pretty good lately.

We have two little girls who have both decided that going potty on the potty is a pretty great thing. I have gone for daaays without changing a stinky diaper, and this alone makes me less afraid of getting out of bed in the morning.

We have a little boy who has not had an "askident" for weeks. He often grins and announces, "No wadder...no askident!" before bedtime and we are overjoyed that he now understands the relationship between clear water going into the body and yellow water coming out of it.

We have a bigger boy who is learning to read and play the piano beautifully. He turns seven soon and continues to be the bigger and wiser (though still slightly younger) brother to Andrey and Reagan. He has navigated the weirdness wonderfully and I love his fluffy red head.

We have a big girl who helps her little sisters get dressed in the morning and make their beds. She is also playing the piano beautifully and composing her own music. Her wavy, freehand, handwritten staff on the paper thrills me.

We have a biggest boy who is reading *The Lord of the Rings* and *Plutarch*, and learning geometry in sixth grade that I never learned in tenth grade. I thought I lost him in Costco last week but he reassured me that no harm could come to him because, don't you know, he had his pocketknife.

There are still so many unknowns and surprises. The other day I found a magnet stuck to Reagan's head, and my first thought was, "Oh, Jesus!!!" and then (I'll be honest) my next thought was, "Well, that explains a lot." I was trying to figure out whether I should call the doctor or our attorney first when I realized it was stuck to her barrette.

Happy anniversary to us. We've been home, all eight of us, all together, for good, forever, for six months. I think we're going to make it.

Dear kids, I posted on social media, *We have successfully scheduled our 6-month post-adoption home visit with the social worker. Please don't tell her about the jousting, the gun I got for Christmas, or that time I took pictures of Iree hanging upside down from a tree before I helped her unsnag her snowpants. Thanks.*

Our six-month visit required gathering photos and checking documents, and we realized we needed to send a family photo to the Powers That Be in Bulgaria because they wanted to know what we looked like.

It took some work, as you can probably guess. We used the timer on our little click-and-shoot camera, arranged ourselves with the woods as a backdrop, and took turns running full-tilt from the deck, skidding across the sidewalk, and leaping over the snowbank and up the hill in less than ten seconds so we could compose ourselves with dignity as though we'd been waiting patiently for, oh, *minutes*, before the camera clicked.

If you saw the string of photos we ended up with, you'd notice that one of us doesn't care to be in front of the camera at all. We get the stinkface, the I'm-being-poisoned face, and the blurry bolting-out-of-the-picture action shot all the time. But he could be bribed with chocolate chips.

I couldn't figure it out. Nothing happened to him when we took his picture, but he cringed every time, convinced it should be avoided at all costs. We're a lot alike in some ways. He's my biological son; he looks like me. I remember doing the same thing too when I was younger...sometime last year. (Kidding. I was probably his age and I vividly remember hiding behind my favorite dog at Grandma's house whenever someone had a camera.)

Actually, I was the same way the week before we prepped for the home visit. Not cringing from photos, but from loud noises because I was sick for two days with an awful headache and dizziness, and spent those forty-eight hours mostly on the couch or in bed between staggering trips to the bathroom. No one else had it, just me, and every noise made me cringe – a kid yelling, a chair scraping across the floor, a dish clinking. Everything made my head pound.

For days afterward, I still flinched whenever there was a loud noise. The headache was gone, I was all better, there was no threat, but I had gotten used to cringing from noise and it had turned into a habit.

I realized it was similar to what Reagan did when I brushed her hair. Even when all the tangles were out and the brush went through smoothly, she jerked away and whimpered like it hurt. It was a habit. She'd been hurt before and knew what it was like, and she thought it might happen again. The pain probably wasn't real, but the fear of it was.

A couple of days after I was healthy again, Reagan kept dropping a heavy toy repeatedly during quiet time. Andrey was napping, the big kids were doing assignments, and I was still cringing from the headache that finally wasn't there. I told her to put away the toy and find something quiet. She dropped the toy again, on purpose. And then she did it *again* on purpose. I caught a flicker of a smile, and she knew that I knew that she knew she was disobeying. She went to timeout, and the toy went on the counter.

A couple of minutes passed. She was calm and sitting in the corner. I picked the toy up off the counter and repeated, "Reagan, you need to put this away" and as I bent over to give it to her, she threw her arm over her face, cringing and shuddering. She cowered, afraid I was going to hit her with it. I hadn't seen her flinch like that since we brought her out of the orphanage, and she shrank into the corner, feeling a very real fear of someone who was no threat to her at all.

Six months was not long enough to convince her that this new female, this mommy-person, was safe to be around when she knew she was in trouble.

How do you rebuild trust after so much pain?

We talked with the social worker about that and many other things during our visit. She asked if we thought Reagan and Andrey understood the adoption or the concept of family, and we didn't know. (Was this a pass/fail quiz? We didn't know that, either.) We suspected they thought our house was just a really nice, small orphanage with only two grownups called Mommy and Daddy. Every adult around them was a potential mommy or daddy, and in those early years, it was evident they would jump at the chance to trade us out.

Reagan struggled with obedience, trust, balance, motor skills, and coordination, and as I mentioned, all these came into play at the top of a new set of stairs. She knew she could hold the rail or hold our hands, and take her time about it. But if a well-meaning person came along and *took* her hand without asking us after we told her to hold the rail, suddenly Reagan was picking out a new Mommy or Daddy, and it wasn't us. It was triangulation: two steps forward on the stairs, twenty steps backward in her healing. This kind of help was like pouring gasoline onto a fire. Just because it's wet doesn't mean it puts the fire out.

(We interrupt this chapter for a very important Public Service Announcement. If you see an adoptive family you know in public, please do not "help" the parents with their adopted children in any way without discreetly asking first. Failure to do so may result in outbursts, snappishness, dirty looks, and major fallout afterward...not to mention how the children might respond.)

"But she needs to learn to trust other people, too," we heard. Nope, she didn't. She would have gone home with any stranger who gave her a fake smile; trusting strangers was clearly not the issue. *She needed to learn to trust her parents and obey them.* Navigating relationships with other people had to wait. She needed to know she belonged to a special group of people called "family." Regardless of race or birth or features, she belonged in the picture with us.

But how do you teach that after years of trauma? How do you convince someone they no longer have to flinch? There are no easy answers.

She needed to know that she was safe, loved, and valued, and those concepts were as alien to her as family was. We led her to the stream, the living water that was deep and wide and washing all of us. Someday we wanted her to look into that water and see the One who says, *You're My daughter. You look like Me.*

6: the underwear strikes back

Spring here in Alaska is fleeting and unreliable, coming in fits and starts. By March we know we can count on several more snowfalls and probably at least one more cold spell as the weather hems and haws its slushy way through until we're dried out and blooming again, sometime in May. Forty degrees in March feels wild and free without hats and mittens, though, and I took two of the girls to a local ice cream joint because Iree had earned a special treat.

For just over six dollars we ate mint chocolate chip and fireweed honey, and chatted with tourists. One of them asked if I recommended the ice cream. Another one asked if the honey here was made from fireweed. Then they asked what fireweed jam tastes like, and what the heck a lingonberry is. They asked how long I'd lived in Alaska. They asked if I was born here. I was tempted to point out the rack of bumper stickers on the counter that said, *"Alaska is FULL. I hear the Yukon is lovely, though."*

Really though, they were nice. Then they mentioned they were sad to be leaving because it looked like it was almost spring here.

"Well, our spring isn't really 'spring,'" I apologized, "it's muddy and gross for a long time. It smells bad and looks terrible."

She nodded with condescending expertise. "Oh, I know. It's just like that at home, in Pennsylvania."

Oh. Of course. Yes, I'm sure it's *just* like that three thousand miles away, pardon me. Smile, wave bye-bye, and leave. Just like that, easy.

Everyone wants to be an expert. Everyone wants a little respect for knowing something. We're all guilty; usually it's harmless. But sometimes it's not.

Our kids had weekly swimming lessons, and right next door to the pool was a place our social worker had mentioned as a possible resource for adoptive families. So while Vince and most of the kids were in the lesson, I stopped in with Chamberlain and Reagan to check it out. The receptionist looked up and smiled.

"Hey," I said, "we finalized our adoption six months ago. I just wanted to look around here, is that okay?"

"Are you having any problems?"

That was a loaded, impossible question. I had no idea how to answer. *Well, two kids collaborated to knock my coffee across my laptop, I'm facing childhood fears I thought were dealt with decades ago, and I don't know what to think of my life right now but I'm only afraid to get out of bed every other morning...so yeah, things are pretty great.*

Instead, I fumbled with, "No...not really...well, just the normal stuff. Whatever normal is, anyway." I forced a smile, hoping she understood.

She didn't. But it was worse than not understanding; she knew everything already, and there was no correcting her.

"Six months home? Oh, you're just *fine*. You're still in the honeymoon! Let me show you the library we have here."

"Actually, our honeymoon was over after three days with one of them, and we never had a honeymoon with the other," I said. *Unless the two-hour drive from the orphanages to Sofia counts,* I thought.

She looked at Chamberlain, and didn't even try to hide rolling her eyes at my response.

"No, you're still in it. Trust me. Just wait, it'll get worse." Then she talked to me about books for adopting toddlers, and adopting from Russia. She never asked how old the children were, where we adopted from, how many other children we had, or let me get a word in edgewise. She assumed the children I had with me were both adopted and both toddlers, and since they were both white, we obviously had adopted from Russia.

I smiled. At least, I think I did, but it was probably one of those nauseated smiles husbands give when their wives ask, "Do I look fat in this?" and they know there's no safe answer.

When she finally took a breath, I took advantage of the pause to ask, "Have you adopted?"

She straightened up a little. "Um, no. No, I haven't. But I've done guardianship. Yep, I've been through it *allll* with attachment."

Yes. Yes, of course you have. *Except you haven't*, I thought, and left. Smile, wave bye-bye, and leave. But it felt like I'd been puked on by someone who was supposed to be there as a resource, and instead was there only to inflate her own ego.

We assume so much, and often know so little. How do we walk in grace without allowing people to trample us?

Around that time in an extremely rare situation, Vin was scheduled to work until the wee hours of the morning. I knew I would be going to bed alone. I made the best of it and thought I'd get some writing done, and go to bed at a reasonable hour...say, 1:00 a.m.

But I'm not responsible enough to put myself to bed at a reasonable hour. I ended up writing and eating ice cream until 3:00 am. And I felt safe. Few things could be more terrifying for an intruder to stumble upon than an Alaskan woman on a sugar high wearing an avocado mask, with a .44 in one hand and her knitting needles in the other.

That year we'd been on our toes, tightly sealed, and on alert for months. It wasn't just because of everything we were going through post-adoption; we were on the lookout and on our knees for someone who had been intruding into safe places, demanding more grace than most of us had left. I did not want him to show up when my husband was not there.

I was reading Ecclesiastes (which a woman should probably never do while PMSing, but alas) and something finally made sense when nothing else had been:

> *But all this I laid to heart, examining it all, how the righteous and the wise and their deeds are in the hand of God. Whether it is love or hate, man does not know; both are before him.*
>
> *– Ecclesiastes 9:1*

Both were before me, and I did not know.

Some people are insincere, intrusive, and presumptuous, lacking boundaries and fishing for camaraderie. They willfully put themselves in a corrupt situation that hurts others, and then they seek acceptance and even hope for approval. If they're lucky, what they get is grace. I don't think most of them even know the difference.

My heart knows the difference, though. And my heart feels better when I am giving grace and forgiveness instead of giving in or getting even. And grace looks different in different circumstances. For example, in some cases we can smile and nod, and that's grace.

In other cases, we can decide ahead of time that if a certain situation occurs, we will make every effort to aim judiciously and...well, only shoot the intruder in the leg, instead of a more vital area. And that's grace, too.

```
March 14, 2013

All three bathrooms are occupied. The
crud has hit our house.
```

In the middle of the night Vince got up with Cham, who went to bed with the sniffles and woke up with a bad dream. Five minutes later, Reagan was also crying and it was my turn to assist.

Except usually I didn't have to take a turn. The only other time she'd woken us in the middle of the night was right after we got home from Bulgaria, and she was sick then, too, but she screamed when I tried to comfort her. I tried to help her blow her nose and she panicked; I urged her to take a drink of water and she sobbed. The more things I tried, the worse she got. The only way I could comfort her was to give her distance, so I stood outside the room and listened to her cry herself to sleep.

But this time, she called me mama. I helped her blow her nose and she cooperated. I put tea tree oil on her feet and she laid back, safe and content. As I shut the door, she said, "Ni-night, Mama..." and fell asleep happy, not quite seven months later.

Exactly a year earlier we were meeting Andrey for the first time. And now in our part of Alaska, I woke up to similar weather, bare branches waving in a pale grey sky.

The year before, we heard Andrey say two sentences on his own, maybe. This week, this year, he was getting in trouble for having his favorite stuffed animal on the table at mealtimes and arguing about it. "But Koosten is huuungry! See? Koosten saying," – insert squeaky voice - "I'm hungry!"

Around this time the year before, Chamberlain was just learning to speak and Iree was the only one who could reliably interpret what she was saying. But now, things were clearing up: An eye was an eye, an "oo" was an ear. And she reveled in her new ability to pronounce the L sound with a flourish.

"Llllook!" she said at the lunch table, holding up her sandwich: "It's a dwagon!" Another bite. "Oh! Now it's a lllion!" Another bite. "It's a kitty, with two oos!" Another bite. "Oh, a kitty with one oo!" (Poor kitty.)

A year earlier, I thought we had a pretty good handle on potty humor. But fast forward to this week when I asked a certain child to add eighty-seven plus five. He started to answer, "Ninety–" when he was interrupted by musical noises that can only be produced by small boys after eating too much chili.

And his older brother was happy to answer for him: "Ninety-toot."

```
March 19, 2013
```

I cut Reagan's hair. She still writhes and yelps every time we brush it, she can't or won't brush it herself, and it often has food in it because she uses it as a napkin. I've never cut my daughters' hair short before. But I've never had a daughter like her, either.

She has this thing about pretending to chew. Maybe the orphanage workers chewed gum? Usually it's nothing but sometimes there actually is something in her mouth – a few minutes ago it was a small rock. This is the same child who chews erasers (and sometimes crayons), and got caught licking a sponge she was supposed to be wiping the table with. Vincent just found her brushing the wall with her toothbrush.

This was right after she put a bead up her nose, on the same day she discovered the doorbell.

> Iree is reading about Helen Keller, and she reminded me that Helen was six or seven when Anne Sullivan started to work with her…and I am greatly encouraged by that.

This was probably the worst season for Vince to be commuting into Anchorage and gone sixty hours a week, but we kept Saturday nights sacred for our weekly date night. We couldn't leave the house together, of course, but we put the kids to bed and then had a late dinner and movie to ourselves. So it was bliss, almost.

But not that spring.

The food was amazing – we learned to make homemade calzone, and kept trying to master honey sesame chicken. But the movies were different. They weren't entertainment; they were *important*, and it felt like we'd enrolled ourselves in some unintentional curriculum, opening our eyes to more of what needed our attention. Each time, I both dreaded and looked forward to the growth.

We were both justice students in college, and in those less discerning days we had read, watched, and studied unspeakable criminal history. But seeing the depravity of man and lack of answers in secular humanism is actually what led Vin to Jesus, and as we've gotten older and wiser, we've also gotten more critical about what we allow into our home and our minds.

These movies were hard, along the lines of *The Stoning of Soraya M.,* which we had seen a few years earlier. And they weren't movies I'd recommend to everyone, nor did I agree with everything in them. But they broadened us and the Lord used them to pivot the direction of our future: We watched the history of the Japanese invasion of China, the more recent use of child soldiers in Africa, and the modern history of sex trafficking in America and the globe.

And here's the theme from it: all Why do so many elements of our culture teach men that women and children are commodities to profit from, exploit, and dispose of when inconvenient? Why does our culture not only put up with this cheapening, but often justifies and promotes it?

But no, wait, this is America. We don't stone and otherwise brutally victimize women here, we don't recruit child soldiers here, and slavery was outlawed a century and a half ago.

Except it *is* here. In America.

How bad will it have to get before we have enough of this and decide to raise a generation of sons to be real men, and daughters who will accept nothing less?

Our culture convinces women they are too weak and helpless to deal with pregnancy or childbirth, so to contrive a counterfeit power they allow their unborn children to be slaughtered by doctors for profit. Our politicians give it a thumbs-up in exchange for votes, hailing themselves as champions of human rights and women's issues, passing laws that protect predators and pedophiles, while the women they've victimized wonder when their child's birthday would have been and bleed from their vitals. But it's not called any of that. It's called "choice." Slavery was called "choice," too.

Will we decide to raise a generation who will know their worth, unintimidated by creeps who are only interested in consumption and disposal? Our girls need to know that they are not take-and-trash. Our boys need to know that the safety of others is worth battling for. Heroes will fight for their protection so cowards can't prey on their exposure.

Our girls shouldn't sit in the middle of the crossfire and just wait to be rescued, though. Our girls need to know that their femininity is not something to apologize or atone for, that pregnancy is not a disease, and that motherhood is a role of honor, victory, and battle. Our girls need to know that they are not a program to be bought or sold for an evening, a vote, or a salary, *because they are priceless.*

I struggled through it all as our eyes were vividly opened to more of what we had already been learning about. We knew at least one, maybe both, of our adopted children had been headed for such a future, until God intervened and chose us to be the intervention.

The wake-up call was a brief dose of oxygen when it felt like the air had been sucked out of our home. It didn't change any of the pain, or exhaustion, or trauma. But it was a brief lift from the downward spiral that reminded us to love our kids fiercely so they will love others fiercely, to teach them to recognize frauds instead of falling for them, and to instill in them that they, too, are meant to champion a better culture, just like their parents were trying to do.

```
April 12, 2013

    Praising God for the small things: Bis-
cotti hidden in the armoire. A sunny spot
on the couch with tea, where I can see
Andrey out one window and the rest of the
kids out the other. And the relief that
follows panic when you step in something of
questionable texture, only to realize it's
just a rubber toy.
    Attachment is such hard work. Oliver
Twist is a sweet myth of goodness and pur-
ity, and the Cuthberts were spoiled with
Anne of Green Gables. We've got kids put-
ting soap on other kids' toothbrushes, and
kids accusing other kids. We're fighting
for mental health with prayer, encourage-
ment, vitamins, and nutrition. It often
feels like surviving instead of thriving,
and I so want to thrive.
```

The snow outside piled up almost as fast as the neglected books on my to-read list; the woodstove was glowing and smoke drifted west from our chimney. A late snowstorm came in April and people called it Merry Springmas.

The weather alerts kept coming:

```
...WINTER WEATHER ADVISORY FOR SNOW
REMAINS IN EFFECT UNTIL NOON TUESDAY...
  * LOCATION...MATANUSKA VALLEY.
  * ADDITIONAL SNOW ACCUMULATION 3 TO 7
INCHES THROUGH NOON ON TUESDAY.
  * SNOW WILL INCREASE THIS EVENING.
SIGNIFICANT SNOW ACCUMULATIONS WILL PERSIST
THROUGH TUESDAY MORNING. MINOR ADDITIONAL
ACCUMULATIONS OF SNOW ARE POSSIBLE THROUGH
TUESDAY NIGHT.
```

According to officials, that snowstorm made nine consecutive months of snow for Anchorage. The current forecast called for homemade soup and bread for dinner, followed by a 70% chance of Christmas cookies.

The total at our house was seventeen inches – less than some, more than others. The grill out on the deck wore a chef's hat of snow and our cats curled up together like quotation marks inside where it was warm. The kids practiced their theatrical skills in the yard, burying themselves and yelling for help as they pretended to drown in the snow.

The streets had been dry just a few days earlier when the oldest kids had school testing. When it was all over, we had a celebratory lunch with my dad at our favorite cafe, and the waitress introduced me to Greek coffee.

"Greek coffee?" I asked her. "What makes it Greek?"

"Well...I've heard people say it's like sixteen cups of coffee in one cup."

"I'll take one of those." I just like watching my dad's eyebrows go up.

But then this storm hit, and then the snow had to melt all over again, falling off the trees like glacial calving when the sun hit it. And that week we had a different sort of testing.

At a routine medical appointment on Monday, the doctor and nurse doted on Andrey for the entire 30-minute gig in spite of my warnings and he milked it for all it was worth. For example, if a child acts like he's *limping* right after a blood draw, you can bet he is practicing his, ah, theatrical skills, also.

We reaped the consequences all week, and not even Greek coffee could have kept me going any longer than that. I was drowning, and it wasn't until Saturday that the lying, manipulation, and destruction abated to their pre-appointment levels.

The kids were doing chores, I was making oatmeal. We were late; breakfast on Saturday leisurely turned into brunch. The girls were ready, like always, waiting at the table. The boys, like always, were still raising a ruckus in their room, finishing their chores and getting ready to vacuum. Except for the last few minutes, which had been... quiet. Strange. That should've been the tip off.

The stillness was suddenly broken by music blaring from upstairs, from the boys room, as loud as the stereo would go, playing the Imperial Death March from *Star Wars*. Afton solemnly marched toward us, then past us, on his way to the laundry room, with his right arm extended out in front, a pair of dirty underwear dangling from two pinched fingers so as to to keep the offending article as far away from the rest of his body as possible. I guess it's kind of fun to live with a soundtrack.

Underwear was a big deal in our house though because we had three kids in different stages of potty training. Fortunately, only one of them was fluent enough in English to talk about it much. Our three-year-old informed me that even though she couldn't read *Fancy Nancy* yet, due to days-of-the-week undies she could read underwear. The piano teacher and anyone else who would listen frequently got an earful about potty charts, flushing, and how many squares of toilet paper you're supposed to use. (It was also around this time that I began undergoing regular interrogation about this business of mommies and daddies not having to wear jammies – footie or otherwise – at bedtime, and why baby boys had sticky-outy parts and baby girls were...you know, normal.)

So many questions, and I still don't know the answers.

"What is God's wast name?" Cham asked.

"I dunno. I don't think He has a last name."

"He *doesn't*?!" Incredulous disbelief. "Does *Jesus* have a wast name?"

"I don't think so." I considered whether or not I could get away with saying "Josephson" but decided not to. There was no time though, because the questions kept coming fast and furious.

"What was dat wady's name? Miss Cowzone? She came here in her car?"

"I'm not sure..." I stalled. *Who do we know that she would call Miss Calzone...calzone...*

"She had dark hair and a dark car."

"Oh!" Eureka, I knew this one. "Miss Sonya?" The social worker, from the post adoption home visit.

"Oh, yes! Miss Pasagna." This, from the same child who thought we brought her adoptive siblings from an enchanted land called Spaghettia.

We made it to lunchtime, and this:

"I don't want to finish my almonds from lunch. Can I not eat dem?"

I know this answer, too. "No, you need to eat them. They're good for you."

But little Cham was undeterred and not afraid to pull out all the stops: "Does *God an' Jesus* have to eat dem, too?" Stumped again.

When Vin finally came home, the weekend was here. The kids had dinner, and we got them to bed in time for our weekly movie date, hurrah and exhale.

The movie was terrible, but the food was good and the company was excellent. The kids were all asleep and we were two-thirds of the way through the film when suddenly Darth Vader's presence was announced by a full orchestra and approximately eight squadrons of Storm Troopers. It was midnight, and the Imperial Death March blared from the boys room.

One boy was screaming, another boy was thinking about screaming, and another boy slept through the entire Imperial Troop invasion, softly snoring, just like he did when the tree fell on our house. At least some things are predictable.

We fumbled in the dark for the volume button, the off button, the electrical plug, the circuit breaker, whatever, and finally, it was quiet. We calmed down all screaming and potential screaming. The cats, those lazy rubber-neckers, wandered in to see what all the fuss was about.

Apparently, while setting the soundtrack for the Great Imperial Underwear March, someone accidentally set the timer to go off again at midnight for an encore presentation of The Underwear Strikes Back.

A whuffly snore erupted from the bottom bunk as we left the room. Still oblivious. Strong, the force was with him. Question him the next day...we did.

7: on the same side

Sick again, crumpled tissues everywhere. I was a little dizzy, head throbbing and floating somewhere near the ceiling, temperature high, eyes watering. A million things to do but I was stuck in one place; even the pen was heavy. A year earlier I would've pushed through, but now the fear of the day ahead and the need for constant supervision over every little detail made half-steam efforts a hazard to everyone's safety.

Vince took the day off and then took the kids to the store so I could rest in a quiet house, alone. Just me on one couch with the white cat at my feet, and the stripey cat on the other couch, laying on top of a mountain of unfolded laundry. We were all equally productive.

But if I could've moved, I would've flown free through the house. I would've folded the laundry, scoured the kitchen, had lunch ready for their return. I would've watered the plants that were wilting. I'd tackle that writing project and balance the checkbook. I would be in a fever to conquer all of the big and little mountains that were neglected while I was sick.

I thought of all these things, and sneezed. Wiped my nose, wiped my eyes, and wiped the agenda. My greatest accomplishment that week was reading *The Princess and Curdie* by George MacDonald.

> *A mountain is a strange and awful thing. In old times, without knowing so much of their strangeness and awful-*

> *ness as we do, people were yet more afraid of mountains. But then somehow they had not come to see how beautiful they are as well as awful, and they hated them - and what people hate they must fear. Now that we have learned to look at them with admiration, perhaps we do not feel quite awe enough of them. To me they are beautiful terrors.*

And I thought, *The mountains around me **are** beautiful terrors.* All these tasks pile up, looming before us when we're unable to do them. Other people have to do them for us, and that's a little terrifying even for those of us who aren't control freaks.

So Vince took the kids out to buy something – I don't remember what it was, but it must've been so necessary that it was worth navigating a big box store with six kids. I remember reaching toward him in fevered desperation: "Don't do it! *You don't have to prove that you're a hero!*" But he did, and survived, and came home in a fever, swearing to never do it again...until the next day, when I was still sick and he took all the kids to a different store.

My energy ebbed and flowed like sunlight on a partly cloudy day. I sat at the foot of a mountain of tasks and stopped there, determined to go the rest of the way up on a different day. The things on my to-do list were beautiful terrors that could be conquered later in the week.

```
April 30, 2013

We spent an entire winter teaching Reagan
how to put on snowgear, and now we've made
it to spring, which only requires boots and
```

a jacket. She can put the jacket on by herself (praise God!), which she couldn't do all winter.

I need to clean while they're all outside. I might even vacuum. It desperately needs done and for once I'm not even hoping that one of the kids will earn an extra chore so I can assign it to them as a consequence. I want them to JUST BE NICE AND GET ALONG, so help me.

It's ten minutes later, and I'm done… though I passed the rest of the vacuuming off to Chamberlain, who still considers it a high privilege.

For some reason, forty-two degrees in May always feels about thirty degrees warmer than forty-two degrees in the fall. The same temperature that makes us shiver in September makes us leave our coats behind and go picnicking in spring. And I know that wherever you are, temperatures are probably different; hot and cold are relative. But for here, where I live, this is how it is. Let me illustrate how we respond to temperatures in Alaska:

-30 to -10 degrees: Very cold. All snow gear required; follow up with hot cocoa encouraged.

-10 to 10 degrees: Pretty cold. Must wear snowgear, but extra socks are optional.

10 to 25 degrees: Chilly. Jackets and hats usually required; mittens necessary if a snowball fight ensues.

25 to 40 degrees (Autumn): Mittens and hats encouraged, snowpants optional. Whining about going outside equals forfeiture of hot cocoa upon reentry.

25 to 40 degrees (Spring): Jackets optional. Look at the icicles melting in the sun! It's a heatwave!

40 to 60 degrees: Anything from tank tops to sweaters is appropriate, depending on windchill. This is particularly superior weather for farmer tans.

60 to 70 degrees: We are running out of ideas for popsicle recipes. Frozen smoothies made from bumper-crop zucchini and strawberries is an acceptable dinner option.

70 to 80 degrees: Men and boys are shirtless, and little girls are asking if they can go shirtless, too. Their mothers are considering, since it saves on laundry.

80 to 100 degrees: Showers and baths are replaced with water fights, garden hoses, and kiddie pools. Blue tarps and pickups are optional but not necessary, unless you live in certain (cough-Butte-cough) areas. Hide in shaded areas and daydream of winter.

The yard was patchy with the last of the snow, and only the faintest bit of green was showing on the trees. It was probably just lichen.

People kept asking how school was going for Andrey and Reagan. The short answer was...they weren't ready for it. School for them looked different; the last eight months had been about learning new routines, limits, and boundaries, along with how to speak English. Teaching math and handwriting wasn't a huge priority; we had to teach them they were safe.

They were learning letters, colors, table manners, and hygiene. How to get in and out of the Stagecoach, and how to buckle a seatbelt. They were learning that Mom and Dad were neither their slaves nor their tyrants. They were safe but not spoiled, and that was confusing, frustrating, and unfamiliar middle ground to both of them. They wrote, colored, drew, and scribbled, but they still needed to learn to hold a pencil correctly. Partly it was motor skills, partly it was a variety of diagnoses, and partly it was that they often did things wrong on purpose because they knew it would command my attention longer.

We planted seeds and our dining room was overrun with sprouting things. Alaska has a short growing season, just a few months of great daylight to cultivate a harvest before the snow flies again. And we started fairly simple, using a little greenhouse method: Small seedlings clustered in the middle of our dining room table, covered by an overturned clear plastic bin to protect them from feline scavengers. We ate meals around it. And then we graduated to seedling pots, and then the project took over the kitchen counter.

We were impatient for growth, for budding. I walked around the driveway with the little girls, kicking snow into the dry areas to help it melt faster. Cham kept asking to hold my hand but let go whenever she found new piles of snow to stomp on, and then she came back to hold my hand again as we walked and crunched and kicked together, all over the yard, all over the driveway.

Suddenly Reagan reached out to me and said, "Mama? Hand?" She had never asked me to hold her hand before, unless she needed help moving somewhere. Maybe she was just copying Chamberlain. Maybe her hands were cold. Maybe it was just lichen...but it was green. It looked like growth to me.

Our garden outside was unimpressive, but I had a different route as a backup plan.

I love avocados. They're expensive here so we don't get them very often, but maybe the real reason we never buy them is because Vince thinks they're disgusting, slimy things that sneak into perfectly good sandwiches and tacos, rendering them completely inedible. So he was not thrilled when he saw an avocado pit balanced in a cup of water, with a sprout coming out of the top of it. Our conversation went like this:

"You're growing an avocado plant?" he asked.

"Um...yes."

"This is Alaska."

"I know."

"Avocados won't grow in Alaska." He's never confessed it, but I suspect this is one of the reasons he moved here.

"It's okay, we're growing it inside. It's science, see?"

"You realize that avocados grow on *trees*, don't you?"

"Mm-hmm. I'll trim it. And it will be...shrubby."

"And it will grow avocados in the house?"

"In five to seven years, maybe."

"You're growing...an avocado tree...in our house, for at least *five years*?"

"Um. Actually..." I looked over at the windowsill, which held two more avocado starts. He followed the direction of my gaze and then fled the kitchen in despair.

Only one of the starts had sprouted so far. It took months to get roots and a shoot, so we were patient with these other two, also. Well, the kids and I were patient. Vince was patient...with me.

We teased each other, but really, we were on the same side. Teasing each other is okay when the trust level is high, and ours was. It had been low before, and it bottomed out at one point, but we had learned to be on the same side and we were trying to teach our kids the same thing. They were learning that trust is something that has to be earned, and once lost, it empties their tank of credence. It takes many deposits of goodness, sensitivity, and honesty to earn it back and refill the tank. And there's no room for teasing in the meantime – or the *mean* time.

We were learning to fight the good fight, and our family had to be a team in ways we'd never had to before with multiple special needs and special circumstances. Some of us got it, and others mutinied, and we fought for unity with prayer, nutrition, communication, and counseling.

We were *for* our kids, not fighting them, even though they often fought us and each other. We wanted to move from the mindset of being *in trouble* to being *corrected in love*, and we all needed to remember it, because we were really on the same side.

We were trying, at least. We still had some convincing to do, like when Chamberlain innocently presented a bug to me:

"Look at the bug!" she said. "Dis is his bottom."

"We don't talk about bottoms," I reminded her.

As incredulous as only a four-year-old can be, she said, "We only talk about bottoms in the *baffwoom*?"

"Yep."

"An' we *don't* talk about bottoms when we're *not* in the baffwoom?"

"Right."

"Not even about *bugs* bottoms?" She paused, noticing my face contort. "Hey! Stop *waffin'* at me!"

"I'm trying!" I squeaked, stifling as much as I could.

"Now you're *fake* waffin' at me!!" she wailed, running out of the room.

We were trying to remember that a gentle correction brings a gentle response, so they would learn that a gentle answer brings a gentle correction. Because we (usually) weren't mad. They weren't perfect, and we weren't perfect, and we were all learning together.

But we couldn't get away from the subject of friendly fire, because it was part of our history lesson that week.

> *The sun went down on a brilliant victory for the Confederates. Yet the night brought disaster for them.*
>
> *Eager to find out what the Federals were doing, General Jackson rode out towards their lines in the gathering darkness...*

> *"The danger is all over," he said carelessly. "The enemy is routed. Go back and tell Hill to press right on."*
>
> *Soon after giving this order, Jackson himself turned, and rode back with his staff at a quick trot. But in the dim light his men mistook the little party for a company of Federals charging, and they fired. Many of his officers were killed, Jackson himself was sorely wounded and fell from his horse into the arms of one of his officers.*
>
> *"General," asked someone anxiously, "are you much hurt?"*
>
> *"I think I am," replied Jackson. "And all my wounds are from my own men," he added sadly.*
>
> *- H. E. Marshall* [1]

Infighting among family, church, and troops, is born of fear and defensiveness. Our deepest wounds come from our own people. But what if our aim was truer because our vision was clear, and we realized we're on the same side?

We would stop letting fear have its heyday with us. We would choose to believe the best in each other. We would trust that He made us for a special purpose. We would realize that we don't need to compromise for anyone else's ideals or insecurities.

> *He will tend his flock like a shepherd; he will gather the lambs in his arms; he will carry them in his bosom, and **gently lead those that are with young**.*
>
> *- Isaiah 40:11*

We would trust that He knows what He's gotten us into. Because He is on our side, too.

May 22, 2013

The older kids are getting along and it's a huge gift because my head is ringing from the squabbling of the little ones. Some days the noise of six kids is nothing, but other days are total cacophony. And I berate myself: When did Gladys Aylward have time for self pity while trekking with a hundred children through the forest in China to escape the horrors of war, while subsisting on soup from boiled leaves and grass?

But on the other hand, she had a breakdown at the end of it.

Some days are fine. Other days I hear the voice of the enemy through the mouths of those who should have supported us, but have chosen to accuse and attack instead. Some days it's harder to fight against discouragement, to remember that I can still be a good mom to all of my kids, that our biological children aren't suffering from bringing Andrey and Reagan home, and I remember that life will get better. That our family's future happiness isn't ruined by welcoming the heartache of two broken children who desperately need healing, and that walking into the suffering of others doesn't destroy our joy, but cements it.

I try to remember that. And I try not to resent those who said otherwise out of their own ignorance and weakness.

I spend the day wiping tables and counters and dishes and bottoms. Wiping my eyes and wiping noses and wiping tears from all of us.

Wow. This is not a very uplifting entry.

I wrote a list on a scrap of paper and I'm keeping it nearby, trying to abide by it:

Just let them have fun.
Include them.
Draw them in, instead of pushing them away.
Don't teach them to isolate.
Teach them joy.
Show them joy.
Be on the same side.

I read the Bible out loud and I push through it, much like I push through the days, not seeing fruit but believing that faithfulness bears fruit anyway. The Word is heard and does not return empty. The day is pressed through, the laundry done, the meals cooked and dishes washed, children taught and loved, and none of that returns empty, either.

Aside from the Bible, I had been mostly reading the wrong things. Not *bad* things, but just books that didn't inspire or provide enough counterweight to the heaviness of our days. It certainly wasn't the books' fault; one of them was an old favorite on homeschooling and motherhood, but this time the same book that had galvanized and encouraged me years earlier left me feeling like a failure this time because...depression, I guess. Homeschooling and motherhood were so different now. Joy was a key to survival now.

So we started reading *Anne of Green Gables*. On the weekends, over a month, I had the utter joy of introducing my whole family to one of my most loved books of all time. It reminded me of the beauty in everyday domesticity and inspired me to do housework. Strange witchery.

I read aloud during dinners, and when I got sick again for a week, Vince took over and read to us.

> *The long platform was almost deserted; the only living creature in sight being a girl who was sitting on a pile of shingles at the extreme end...She was sitting there waiting for something or somebody and, since sitting and waiting was the only thing to do just then, she sat and waited with all her might and main.*
>
> *- L.M. Montgomery* [2]

Some authors can look into a room and describe only the trash, the filth, and the greasy lifestyle (this is why Steinbeck and I are not friends). But there are others who can look in the same room and see the hardworking mother, the hopeful child, and the steaming bowl of broth on the table that, admittedly, probably still needs to have the crumbs and spills from the previous meal wiped off of it (and this is why Dickens and I *are* friends). I was often so caught up in the messes, defiance, pain, and bickering, I forgot to find beauty.

For almost a year I had been focused on the grief and burden of it all. No one reached out to us when we were imploding behind closed doors. Most people didn't understand in the least what we were going through, so I began countering our community's ignorance of our situation with brutal transparency on my blog about how difficult things were, post-adoption. From online adoptive groups I'd heard from hundreds of other families who were drowning right in front of their pro-adoption congregations and communities, and we all needed real support instead of an occasional pat on the back.

At a barbecue at our close friends' house, we spent the evening on high alert as we always did in large groups of people. We intervened when a child hugged a total stranger and wouldn't let go. We pulled a child out of a game for following another adult around instead of actually playing. We held a child after she kept trying to seek attention from another mommy. In the midst of catching up with friends, we were constantly on the lookout for red flags, trying not to make anyone else feel like they needed to walk on eggshells around us. I doubt we succeeded.

As we gathered our crew to go home, an acquaintance stopped me. Over the course of the evening she saw many of the issues we dealt with, and we had talked at length about the gory details while eating barbecue from our paper plates. She smiled at me.

"I just love watching you guys," she said. "You are doing a beautiful thing."

I had forgotten, but her reminder was a gift.

I forgot that two kids who had been fighting hammer and tongs all year were now playing cards and laughing together. I forgot that Reagan, who was mostly non-verbal a year earlier, could now speak in halting English phrases and sometimes even sentences.

After two rounds of holding a raging child, I needed to remember that this, too, was somehow beautiful and redemptive. I needed to remember that our biological children were amazingly gracious. And I needed to remember that every day held great purpose, for great good.

In the middle of suffering, stuck in the chaos and the cacophony, we forget that we are living something beautiful. Sometimes we need a friendly reminder to keep looking for it.

8: make them scour the anchor

May 28, 2013

Cham has been teaching Andrey animals. "Dis is a turkey," she says. "A turkey is a bird, but you eat it." Andrey remains in scandalous disbelief: "Nooo, dat's gwoss!!"

We made bacon-wrapped jalapeños and I secretly wished that Reagan would try to sneak one of the many jalapeño seeds that were scattered all over the counter to cure her of scavenging crumbs. But no such luck, and about ten seconds later I squirted jalapeño juice in my eye. I yelled "Oh, Jesus!" as the searing pain hit. Lord, have mercy on me, a wretched sinner.

My head was bowed, my eyes were closed. Tears were welling and the Spirit was moving mightily. But in the midst of worship, I felt the slightest tickle of a mosquito trying to make itself comfortable on my raised arm and I creamed that sucker into oblivion without shame or hesitation while singing "Bless the Lord, Oh My Soul."

But with her sensory issues Reagan didn't seem to feel the mosquitoes, and she was so covered in bites that we called it the mosquito pox. Sometimes she would seemingly overreact from little things like a person brushing against her, but she didn't seem to notice temperature changes and she didn't care about scratches from walking through the woods.

Her siblings were a different story, of course. When one of the girls crashed her bike and came in the house with road rash, she was...well, to paraphrase Johnny Cash, she was a-shrieking and a-crying in the mud and the blood and the tears. To make it worse, she was faced with a mama holding peroxide, and she asked the dreaded question:

"Will it hurt?"

I decided to just pour it on and answer later. It's entirely possible that amid the bloodcurdling screams that followed, she never heard me say "Yes."

Sometimes it's better not to ask. We're face to face with the remedy, the Lion standing at the stream we're thirsting for, and we know the answer. Of course it will hurt.

What we are really asking is, *Do I have to?*

And we don't have to, always. We can refuse to take it, refuse to feel it, refuse to soak and let our colors deepen. Some seasons of pain just roll through like waves, and you know another one is about to crash. We can choose infection instead. But there is no other stream, and our dry places will stay thirsty unless we run to Him again and again, soaking in the water and coming out stronger.

We were outside on the rug, on the picnic hill, on a dry brown lawn, in 70 degrees. Our feet were bare, our socks discarded in a pile next to us. Spring had already brought rain, flooding, and ducks, followed by a late snow, and now we had this beautiful summer weather. Trees that were naked in the morning unfolded their leaves by the afternoon. We interrupted a planned assignment to examine a freshly killed mosquito under the microscope. We finished *Oliver Twist* and *Ten Apples Up on Top*. We walked to the mailbox. Homeschooling was the most natural thing in the world for us, but old routines that used to work had to be set aside for what was actually working. Maybe we'd pick up the old ways and dust them off later, after the dust actually settled. And so much was unsettled.

Our whole family changed doctor's offices. The provider who had been enthusiastically supportive through the entire adoption process discovered that the reality of post-adoption is not glitter and rainbows, and the boundaries Andrey and Reagan required cramped her style. Her ego was sore at being confronted with handling them poorly – she was also the kind of doctor who got offended if you requested a second opinion – but instead of apologizing and learning from the experience, she said, "Maybe our office just isn't right for them." And in that, at least, she was correct. All eight of us switched to a different clinic, and I knew it would be better in the long run but it felt like starting from scratch.

Starting over is hard but so necessary, in so many ways. I needed to go back and remember who I wanted to be, back when I dreamed of being a mom of many.

And really, I don't remember what exactly those dreams were, but I know they didn't involve children knocking over my coffee and spilling it all over my laptop.

I told myself that it was already old in laptop years, and death by coffee was really the most merciful way for it to go. So we got a new one and ~~I tried really, really hard~~ I sort of tried to learn how to use it.

But I wasn't happy about it. The icons looked funny and the email was ugly. The word processing program was weird and the photo editing program worked differently. Things that were streamlined for the sake of efficiency didn't feel very efficient when my fingers kept looking for the "end" key but hit "delete" instead – or worse, the insert key. (*I despise you, Insert Key.*) I spent forty-five minutes fighting a battle with HTML and won, briefly felt like a genius, then spent forty-five seconds trying to plug the cord into the wrong side of the laptop. Nothing was normal, and I raged and cried in frustration more than once.

Everything was already so unfamiliar. But what was really changing was my expectation of what things were supposed to look like.

June 28, 2013

What surprises me about the difficulty of adoption is not so much how the new circumstances are so hard to deal with – we knew it would be hard – but how it's revealed the hardness in my own heart and mind. And that has been the most painful thing to realize. In spite of all the training, my heart still expected more positive feelings after adopting. I never expected life to look this way. I am still searching for the beautiful in what often feels so ugly.

And yet.

A simple phone call with a difficult family member is enough to remind me that we really are living a beautiful life. A glimpse of a lifetime of anger, resentment, disorder, hatred, laziness, and lies reveals an instant, vivid contrast that is a painful but necessary wake up call for me. I don't ever want to become that. I don't want my kids to have anything to do with that lifestyle. And I need to remember the contrast without letting the aftertaste of bitterness stick to my thoughts afterward.

This year has pushed me toward writing, praying, and unpacking filth that I didn't know was inside me. Unpacking lies I've believed and wounds I thought were healed long ago. C.S. Lewis said, "No man knows how bad he is till he has tried very hard to be good," and he's right. [1]

God is bringing so much to the surface – piece by piece, peace by peace – and He brings His order and wholeness to each one as we tackle it together. On the surface, some things seem too small to bother praying about, but when I do, suddenly they're exposed as the tip of something long buried under pain that was planted long ago. He's setting things in order that I didn't even know were messy, and when I write it out, it starts to make sense.

I've been reading Jeremiah. Here:

> *Circumcise yourselves to the Lord;*
> *remove the foreskin of your hearts, O men of Judah and inhabitants of Jerusalem;*
> *lest my wrath go forth like fire, and burn with none to quench it, because of the evil of your deeds."*
>
> *– Jeremiah 4:4*

And He says to me, *Remove what is destined to burn so the fire does not come near you when I light it. Create a backfire.*

One of the main things destined to burn was fear – in both me and our kids, in big things and little things.

For example, baking bread used to be so intimidating to me. It was unfamiliar territory and seemed like a big process; I wasn't sure if I really wanted to tackle it. But once I did tackle it, I got a little braver. I learned to play.

There's something instinctively comforting about feeling the warmth of risen bread dough against your hands when it's soft and puffy, like toddler cheeks. I love folding in mozzarella and sautéed onions with so many herbs they fall out and sprinkle the counter when you lift the dough onto the baking sheet. I love the *pfff* sound when you punch the dough down after the first rise, and the act of dividing it into little loaf portions and tucking them into their pans. I love watching it rise.

I kept trying new things and discovered the love of stretching strips of pizza dough over calzone filling, rolling long, thin triangles into crescent rolls, and layering other strips of dough together with cinnamon sugar in between. Then we learned to make doughnuts, and I loved cutting out floury circles, and – the best part – little floury doughnut holes. Oh, joy! Oh, bliss! Oh, dentist!

Playing is messy but so essential. We need it from the earliest of ages. When we're little and don't have enough play, touch, and interaction, many things that should just be routine are anxiety-provoking, unfamiliar territory. And then fear comes into play, literally. We learned a little – just a tiny bit – about this during some of the adoption trainings. But as it usually happens, we learned quite a bit more through actual experience.

The first time we saw fear come into play was when we met Reagan. We gave her some play dough – because all kids like play dough, right? – and when she squeezed it, she cried. We thought, *Hmm, that's weird*, and found different toys to play with.

But after a year of being home together, trying new things and learning more and more, there still didn't seem to be any hard and fast rules about sensory issues. "Not all symptoms or characteristics may be present," one resource said. "A child can be both hypersensitive and hypo-sensitive." And I love this: *"Inconsistency is a hallmark of every neurological dysfunction."* Well, thanks so much. That's just great.

So we played. So many things were new and intimidating, and we focused on making those things familiar so fear would have less unfamiliarity to hold on to. It took a year, but she finally loved play dough. And not just for eating. (Kidding. She only ate it twice...I think.) Messy creativity, textures, temperatures, movement, sound – it was all sensory play. Of course, we never called it that before. We just called it *normal* play. But now we didn't take it for granted.

> ...My object is to show that the chief function of a child – his business in the world during the first six or seven years of his life – is to find out all he can, about whatever comes under his notice, by means of his five senses; that he has an insatiable appetite for knowledge got in this way; and that, therefore, the endeavor of his parents should be to put him in the way of making acquaintance freely with nature and natural objects.
>
> - Charlotte Mason [2]

We'd learned from hiking that splinters didn't faze Reagan at all but, as I mentioned, that was not the case with the rest of her siblings. Chamberlain came downstairs one night after bedtime with a splinter, and after several minutes of Vince and I taking turns with the tweezers amid her shrieks and tears, it was unavoidable – the dreaded implement had to be used. You know the one: The fearsome sewing needle.

I handed her a stuffed animal and found myself saying, "I think Pup has a splinter, too. How about you check him with the tweezers —" putting those worthless things in her right hand "— while I look at your splinter a little more?"

It was a prompting of the Holy Spirit, and it worked. She was engrossed in Pup's right paw, oblivious while I held her left hand poking at it with the needle to expose the end of the splinter.

She was jabbering away to Pup (about how he must be more careful in the woods around the rosebushes) when I asked her if we could trade. She looked at me with surprise but handed me the tweezers while she continued Pup's surgery with the needle. One more pinch and the tweezers grasped the splinter, and we looked at it together. Out in the open, it was just a tiny little thing, and she toddled back to bed.

Then the Lord told me, *You are the one holding Pup.*

I almost dropped the tweezers. *What?*

He said, *As you learn about these kids, all six of them, and you look for their owies that need healed and the things they need to learn, and you kiss them and cry over them and are engrossed in their need for restoration and growth...I am holding the needle. I am working on you.*

There were wounds and impurities inside me, and He was calmly, carefully, quietly pulling them out as I jabbered on and on to Him about all the pups I was holding. Things that used to intimidate me were almost normal now, and I hardly noticed because my attention was focused on these kids and their needs.

God was exposing and removing things that fueled fear, shame, and pride. As I yielded to His work, He was creating a backfire: a new, intentional fire started in the path of an oncoming one, so as to use up the fuel ahead of time and create a barrier of safety that the uncontrolled fire could not cross. He was clearing a path to remove flammable areas of my life. They could burn under His control as I surrendered, or they could burn out of control later.

Either way, they were destined for the fire.

And He's still doing it. As we teach and comfort our kids, He is still pulling things out, continually refining us and exposing little and big things that cause pain. He brings them out into the open so we can look at them together. And then He sends us off, free, showing us new ways to play so we can be anxious for nothing because He loves to watch us rise.

A fascinating thing about boys: five seconds after you tuck in their angelic little faces, you close the door, get half a step away from their room, and utter bedlam breaks loose.

Almost every night, it was the same thing. *No talking,* I told them. *No goofing off,* I told them. *And absolutely, under no circumstances, no wrestling,* I told them.

Smiling nods. Suppressed giggles. I was prepared. I shut the door...waited...and kaboom, it was like someone set off Roman candles while simultaneously high diving off the bunk bed.

So we'd had enough. After several unheeded scoldings during a wild rumpus in their bedroom, we sent them outside to kill mosquitoes while they worked off their energy. You're welcome, Wasilla.

We had them pull weeds, do push ups, scrub lawn chairs, clean out the rain gutters, anything to help them decide that being in bed was a better idea than the alternatives we could think of. Remember, it doesn't get dark in Alaska until well past midnight in the summer.

> *Moms also need to keep boys' little minds and hands busy. It's in their best interest to do so. My father once said about our energetic toddler,*

> *"If you let that kid get bored, you deserve what he's going to do to you."* Shirley's stepfather, who has a South Dakota accent, once said after babysitting our kids for a week, *"Oh, der good kids. You just gotta keep 'em out in da open."*
>
> – Dr. James Dobson [3]

My grandma raised five boys, and there's a story about one of them – I won't mention names, but (cough) he's the one most closely related to me – who was sitting on top of a cardboard box with his pocketknife, just stabbing the box, over and over. And as he told it to me, the only reason he got in trouble for it was because his little brother was inside the box.

Really, it's a miracle she let him live so I'm even here to tell you about this.

One night with my own boys I was proactive and had two of them run ten laps around the house before bedtime. I didn't expect one of them to take a drink out of the hose somewhere around lap seven, and then decide that his brother also needed a drink...while he was running...and not expecting the full force of thirty-degree water to hit him in the face as he rounded the corner.

The other boy who wasn't running laps was busy with another project because the day before he hid his sister's locket in the teeny-tiny crevice between the floor of our garage and the pavement of the driveway, wedging it in just perfectly so that it fell beyond reach and vision. He made a vague confession that led to thirty minutes of chipping concrete and poking around with a flashlight and a hacksaw blade before Vince emerged victorious with the treasure. So that boy was still carefully refilling the crevice with dirt and doing a few other chores for good measure.

And I thought to myself, *This is beautiful, remember?*

> *This gave me occasion to observe that when men are employed they are best contented; for on the days they worked they were good natured and cheerful, and, with the consciousness of having done a good day's work, they spent the evening jollily; but on our idle days they were mutinous and quarrelsome, finding fault with their pork, the bread, etc., and in continual ill humor, which put me in mind of a sea-captain whose rule it was to keep his men constantly at work; and when his mate once told him that they had done everything, and there was nothing further to employ them about, "Oh," says he, "make them scour the anchor."*
>
> – Benjamin Franklin [4]

So one night, that particular little man was on the back deck. After expressing that he really *wanted* to run laps after bedtime, he learned that not everyone gets the consequence he is hoping for, and he was out there with a commission to get ten mosquitoes. I gave him a yogurt lid to display them on as evidence.

Minutes of whining, sulking defiance, and halfhearted mosquito-swatting passed. He threw the yogurt lid out onto the lawn and declared he wouldn't do it.

And then it started to drizzle, because God loves me.

"Mom!! Iss raining!"

"I know!" I sympathized. "You should probably start obeying soon and get those mosquitoes!" Smile.

Furrowed eyebrows. He was considering it.

A few minutes later I checked on him. He had four mosquitoes on the lid, and he caught my eye.

"Dere's no 'oskeetoes!" he protested, although I could see several hovering around the back of his head, and one of them landed. He swatted, examined his hands, and scraped the remains of his prey onto the lid. Shrugging and pouting, he carelessly tilted the lid as he scanned the horizon for sympathy, for release, for another mosquito – and suddenly he realized what he was doing, and righted the lid quickly, but too late. Back down to four mosquitoes.

He looked through the window, but couldn't see me because I was hiding behind my cat, stifling laughter. He inspected the floor of the deck but sadly, not only was the mosquito that fell off of the lid not there, but no other dead insects had chosen to lie in repose in that exact spot for his sole benefit, either.

Attachment issues were in full play, and as often as he could make eye contact with me he announced he was done with six, then eight, then nine, then eight again, and finally twelve (you heard me mention attachment, yes?) dead or dying mosquitoes. Eventually he put the right number on the lid and was sent to bed without further drama, and I didn't have to drag him (or drug him) to get there. Win.

We were almost to the weekend. We were ready to meet any further disturbance of the peace with orders from friends who needed help lawn mowing, weed whacking, dandelion pulling, driveway sweeping, garden watering, leaf raking, window washing, or any other anchor-scouring they could think of. I told them they could even play the "Imperial Death March" while the boys worked; I'd heard they liked it.

9: scar tissue

July 18, 2013

3:00 a.m. All three boys have been up with bad dreams, crying, and itching, and I've been up with them.

We've suspected for a while that Andrey came home with scabies but our previous doctor insisted it wasn't possible. Afton caught it a few months ago but again the doctor said no, it must be something else; if it were scabies we all would have been infected immediately. Nevertheless, a few weeks ago we realized for sure that's what it was, thanks to internet research and our new doctor. We think the oregano oil we used all winter to fight off colds and flu must have kept the rest of us from catching it earlier.

So now we are daily doing eight loads of laundry, and changing sheets, and covering the furniture, and praying that the rest of us and the cats don't get it. So gross. On top of this, Vin woke up Sunday unable to walk and was in so much pain he couldn't even get into the Suburban until Tuesday to go to the chiropractor, who said he had a slipped disc. He's been able to walk a little since that adjustment, but we don't know when he'll be able to work a full eight-hour shift and manage the hour commute both ways.

And I am run ragged. Overwhelmed, overtired, overworked; my mind plays tricks on me, thinking that since Vin is home I should be able to get more done (as would normally be the case) but of course, this is not the normal case. He is mostly immobile and now it's 3:15 a.m. and I've slept for maybe ten minutes.

God has been putting up with my questions and worries all night about Andrey and Reagan. About trying to find joy and remember purpose and recognize victories. And I asked Him, What have we done? Have we really made a positive difference at all, or have we just made our family life more irritable, bitter, and frustrating? Because I am often struggling. This is not who I want to be.

And He said, *I'm not done yet.* He said it gently, and then He said, *This is healing you.*

I came upstairs with Vin's ibuprofen and one kid's vitamins and my ice cream – we all medicate differently – and Vin said, "I have a word for you."

What, I said.

"You are not a failure." And I cried. He had no idea what I'd been hashing out with God.

It's felt like the dream is deflating, that it's not what I thought it would be and it's all for nothing. And then the enemy hisses, *Well, how has dreaming worked out for you? Are you happy with it?*

And often, the painfully honest answer is, No, I'm not happy. What good have we done here? Are we really helping Andrey and Reagan, or are we just hurting our biological kids and sapping the joy we all used to have?

I know it's just lies from the enemy. But many mornings I don't want to leave the bedroom, and there are many chaotic afternoons when I hear the enemy saying, "I told you so." In the middle of the night I fight bloody hell for joy and peace. I run to Jesus in tears often but not often enough, because He's always willing to wipe them and speak truth. And the truth is, He's not done yet. He is healing each of us. We just had no idea how much healing we needed.

July 29, 2013

Now all the boys have the scabies bumps and we've buckled down, sanitizing and covering both couches, and sitting on the floor instead. We read that you could kill off scabies naturally, so our first days with Vince back to work were consumed with baths, essential oils, and laundry, but we're nervous that the cats might get scabies too, or be harmed by the oils. We throw the windows open and shun the cats' attempts to snuggle. We bought a steam cleaner, and convincing the kids that it's a fascinating new power tool is one of the smarter things I've done in my lifetime. Just like Tom Sawyer, whitewashing the fence.

In the wee hours one morning, I gave up trying to get back to sleep. I was tired, but tired of trying, too.

Another eight loads of laundry were in queue. I thought I'd get some of it done in a quiet house, drink a glass of water, and go back to bed in an hour or so once I was tired enough to fall back asleep.

So I tiptoed downstairs. Two cats, one striped and one solid, came padding behind me. One of them in particular followed me every day. White as a cue ball, she was everywhere I went.

> *Where can I go from my Sophie? Or where can I flee from her presence? If ascend up the stairs, she is there. If I make my bed in the morning, she is climbing all over the pillows. If I take the wash out of the dryer, behold, she is there. If I hide in the remotest part of the house, in the depths of the pantry, even there she will follow me, and her right paw will lay hold of the sandwich I am trying to eat for lunch.*

- Psalm 139:7-10, modified considerably

The girl knew how to abide, to pursue the presence of the one she loved, and to follow the person who loved her best. And I loved that, too – although sometimes I wanted to keep my ice cream to myself.

Despite my grand intentions of getting ahead of the laundry, the clothes in the dryer were still damp. I set it to running again, wondering what to do.

I folded a few blankets. Wiped the counter. Told the cats to be quiet because it wasn't breakfast time yet. I looked for my Bible but couldn't find it. Remembered that it was by the bed, but didn't want to go upstairs to get it.

I grabbed another book instead, and read this:

> *The Spirit must break our practice of the presence of self, and He does this by forging Himself into our inner being. How often these last years have I been filled with that burning? There*

> *were times when I literally felt as though He grabbed my soul with His holy fist and lifted me up before His face with my feet dangling in midair and my tongue protesting, "No, Lord, I can't take anymore. No more, Lord. I'm weary of the painful growth."* [1]

And I realized that the laundry was just a ruse to get me down here to read this, today, right now. Because I needed more of Him urgently.

> *I am learning about those flames which burn but do not consume. I am learning about that fire which releases the odor and fragrance of roses and about that Guest who inhabits the parlor of our souls, who banks the fireplace with ashes to keep the burning low or who uses the billows when the room has grown cold.*

- Karen Burton Mains [2]

I checked the laundry. Pulled out dry things that were wadded around damp towels, and reset the dryer. Folded a pillowcase and some underwear, a set of sheets. It was the Sabbath without rest; Jesus healed on the Sabbath, and we needed healing. But it was quiet and my spirit was resting even when my body wasn't.

Sophie was there, quietly accepting the wait for breakfast, though Gus still loitered in the kitchen. And it was just me and them and Him and the laundry, breathing in peace and fellowship. It was the day of Communion.

The towels were dry and another load went in. I finished folding warm clothes in a cold room, in bare feet on a hard floor. Put away my empty glass. Stacked sheets and towels and underwear, triumphant over another load of laundry, and headed upstairs, two cats following me.

He used His billows to relight the fire, and He banked me in with a down comforter. I fell back to sleep, and He was right there in that place, too.

```
August 19, 2013
```

Reagan walked right into a cold shower tonight and just stood there shivering for several seconds before I realized what she'd done and pulled her out. She's been here for a year, taking showers, but she didn't wait for the water to warm up and didn't think to check the temperature, either. This is a great picture of how she approaches life, and a good reminder of how we need to be teaching her.

Andrey was in full regression for our 12-month home visit, just like he was around our 6-month home visit. Or maybe it never changed.

Our gotcha anniversary came and went with no fanfare and a ton of discouragement. I've heard so much about the joyful celebration of one-year anniversaries, but it is a lie; both our kids are losing ground, refusing to obey over small things that have been routine for a year now: Not asking to be excused from meals. Not speaking clearly. Not flushing the toilet without being told, for crying out loud. And I do want to cry out loud, so help me.

A year earlier, we risked the ocean and stormed two castles and brought two children out of captivity and into a family. For good, forever. It sounded nice – victorious, glorious. But we were walking many places that we did not want to go, and it was a grisly battle.

Over the first year we answered many questions as best we could about how we were doing, and how we thought they were doing. A year later, with some perspective, we were still answering many of the same questions but our answers were a little better than before – not necessarily happier, but more informed, and they all pretty much revolved around the issue of attachment.

Question 1: What are their favorite foods?

Answer: Pretty much everything. One kid would overeat to the point of throwing up, but ironically would also refuse to eat, using a food strike to manipulate and control. It was terrifying. People told us "A child will never starve themselves," but those people have never met a child who is used to starving, and is more hungry for control than food. Another child refused several foods at first but finally came to terms with chicken and eggs and would now eat anything, including food off someone else's unattended plate. We kept the cat food out of reach.

Sandwiches were a novelty that must be eaten in layers – first the top piece of bread, then the inside, and then the bottom piece of bread. Everything had to be smelled first. Fruit was tricky because not all the parts were edible. When I gave Reagan a chunk of pomegranate, she ate part of the bitter rind, screamed, and looked at me like I'd done something cruel to her.

Question 2: How are their English skills?

Short answer: Really great. Andrey picked up English in the first few months and could speak well, though with a thick accent and grammatical errors. Reagan understood it but her speech was still very toddlerish and garbled.

Longer but more honest answer: Much of the garbled pronunciation was intentional. They often refused to say things clearly so you'd ask them to repeat themselves. In the same vein, they also often said "What?" when we spoke to them, not because they didn't hear us, but because they wanted us to repeat ourselves. This was also about attachment; it was a way for them to try to be in control and command our attention for longer. It was also incredibly irritating.

Question 3: What other attachment issues do you face, and what are you doing to remedy them?

And also, questions 4 and 5: What has been the hardest adjustment for you and Vince as parents? What has been the hardest adjustment for the kids?

Never mind. Let's just skip those.

Kidding. But also, question #6: How are you finding healing and redemption through the hard times?

Answer: Um. Chocolate.

And one more, a question we were constantly asking ourselves: When can you come over and play?

I never knew how to answer. Living in a fishbowl is one thing, and displaying open wounds is another. There were things I wanted to tell people that couldn't be said in the clear water of a fishbowl yet, so we waited for scar tissue to form before showing them. The biggest thing we were doing, even twelve months later, was still trying to like them. Surely it should've been easier by now. Surely we should all be attached to each other by now. But they weren't, and we weren't, and we were trying, and the mere fact that it took so much effort felt like failure. A truly nice, good person wouldn't have to work at it so much, right? But it's very hard (and sometimes irresponsible) to believe the best about children who have learned to be sneaky, dangerous, and deceptive as though their very lives depended on it. And in their defense, it's hard for those children to learn to trust adults when they have never known steady, reliable goodness from adults, but instead have suffered at their hands.

The further we went, the more we learned about behaviors we did not pick up on before. Our feelings of continual distrust and jaded skepticism toward them felt wrong, and we hated how the atmosphere had shifted in our home. Their foundational years weren't healthy, so of course their behavior wasn't healthy, but it's also not healthy to live in an environment of constant suspicion, aggression, hypervigilance, and decision fatigue.

It was around this time we learned that adoptive families often endure both primary and secondary trauma, and that parents of children with attachment issues can get PTSD. And we were starting to admit that we were there.

There are some things that it is better to begin than refuse, even though the end may be dark.

– J.R.R. Tolkien [3]

Andrey and Reagan were learning to trust us, and to some extent, we could tell we were making progress because they both fought tooth and nail against it, against us. They were used to temporary, perfunctory relationships with caregivers involving superficial interaction. This was why they seemed to thrive around strangers, acquaintances, and public settings, because the cursory exchange happening on the surface was comfortable for them, like a warm, stinky, full diaper – and equally therapeutic.

Our persistent intimacy in their lives pushed them out of their comfort zone. They much preferred smiling at strangers than holding my hand or answering me when I spoke to them. At church every Sunday they stared at acquaintances and avoided eye contact with Vince and me.

We were here for them, for good, forever, and the nasty unhealthy diaper was coming off, however slowly; they fought and kicked like a baby who didn't want to be changed.

It was hardest when I forgot He was right there in those places with us, but He kept reminding me. This verse was taped to our shower wall in a plastic sheet protector for months:

> *You keep him in perfect peace whose mind is stayed on You, because he trusts in You.*
>
> *- Isaiah 26:3*

But they needed us to like them. Just as God's kindness leads us to repentance, our favor over them brought out goodness that had been buried. Love isn't the issue – we knew that love is a verb, and we chose to love, clean, discipline, smile, supervise, hold, and praise, even when we didn't want to. The real battle was heart-deep, in theirs and ours. Feelings can't be trusted, but they do matter. Winning the battle to like them, to enjoy them, to see the beautiful, is what would make or break us at the end of every day.

10: conduit

September 12, 2013

Just me here, declaring that after I put the kids to bed, I will be back to get some writing in and eat at least three truffles.

The progress so far: Four kids inside, in various stages of bedtime routine. Two boys outside in the rain, in their pajamas, putting away their handmade battering ram, which, praise God, they have not used on the house.

The fern in the woods is turning orange and brown, and the days are drizzly, getting dark outside already. We're fight-ing colds again; Cham is moaning on the couch, just trying to breathe. The teapot is tinkling and humming. I haven't been outside in a week and I'm longing for oxygen, but I also don't want to leave the couch.

Reagan is having a hard week and I'm not sure if it's just the regression cycle or if it's fallout from the dentist appointment on Monday, when the new dentist and hygienist ignored our instructions and babied her. Maybe they got a clue once they saw how uncooperative she was during the exam immediately after.

She walked into a cold shower again today. Last time she did it without thinking, not waiting for the water to warm up, but this time I think she did it because I asked her if it was warm, and she lied and said it was. Lying about obvious things has been her main way of testing limits lately. So I asked her if she wanted to take a warm shower, and she said, "Yes."

"Is this warm?" I asked, feeling it.

"Yes," she answered, smiling and shivering.

I shut the door and refused to play. The water was cool but getting warmer, so she won't freeze but hopefully she'll learn that there are natural (and uncomfortable) consequences to lying.

Lately that's the method we're trying with her in the bathroom. "Did you go potty?" we'll ask, and she'll say yes. "Poopoo or peepee?" we ask, and she'll say poopoo, but when we look, there's nothing there.

"Oh! It looks like you haven't gone poopoo yet. But since you need to go, just sit there until you're done. Take your time!" Force a smile. I think, I hope, it's working. But really I have no idea.

I bless her when she gets out of the shower. "It's nice to have a clean, strong, healthy body. You have a clean, strong, and healthy mind and spirit. God has not given you a spirit of fear, but a spirit of love, power, and sound mind." And she sits on her towel and dries off, smiling. There are so many different things behind those smiles.

Most of the kids were finishing school for the day and I was prepping dinner with two fillets of cold cooked salmon, a bowl of cold mashed potatoes, and a few eggs. I flaked apart the salmon, pulling out tiny elusive bones, making a pile of them on the counter.

Cham was next to me, supervising. "What are you doing? What is that? Why are you doing it that way?" She was four, as if you couldn't tell. My sleeve started to slip down and both of my hands were a mess, so I swiped my arm against my hip to shimmy it back up.

"Mom, can you come look at this?" Her sister, at the table, was having woes with a math problem. I looked across the room at her, and then the project in front of me, and back at her. My eyebrows clearly said, *Are you serious?* but my voice said, "Maybe if you bring it *here.*"

I mixed in the mashed potatoes and some flour, and explained how to borrow from 6000 to subtract 4,536. Threw in a few eggs. This was no job for a spatula and my hands went right in, mixing everything together. The peanut gallery was still watching me, swinging her feet from the barstool.

"Your hands are slimy." She was right. Gelatinous goo from cold fish oil was almost up to my elbows and I pulled my sleeve back up with my teeth.

She slid off the barstool and went to a cabinet. "Are you gonna use dis?"

"Nope, we don't put cocoa in salmon patties."

Another cabinet. "Do you want the big pot?"

"Nope, I'm going to use this pan. Thanks, though." Cutie. But it was time; I needed a break from all the questions so I could get this done.

"Watch out!" I waved my slime-covered hands at her. "I'll get you!" And she shrieked and left, for a few minutes, at least.

She wanted to help and it was adorable. She was not trying to give me advice or run the show; she was just trying to be with me in the middle of it. She would have plunged her hands in the mess with me in a heartbeat if I had given her the chance.

Wouldn't it be nice if that were always the case? We make big life choices sometimes. God's current moves us out of the stream of the status quo and into a new ministry or career, and we get our hands dirty in a deeper calling. And it's awesome until people start questioning our sanity.

"What are you doing? What is that? Why are you doing it that way?" Someone calls an intervention. *You have no idea what you're doing. Please tell me you haven't bought a pair of shiny red knee-high boots and a gold tiara in the last six months. We're going to have to search your closet for bustiers, hot pants, and spandex leggings.*

Suddenly our ability to make choices as independent, successful adults is called into question because we had the nerve to move out of the comfort zone, and it made people around us uncomfortable. Maybe you decided to adopt... again...or have kids...*again*...or move to a different state... or change course entirely. You decided to go deeper. You made some big changes. You radical, you.

We hear about the gossip and conjecture behind our backs. We get the nosy questions to our face. Sometimes it's the smallest of things that bring busybodies out of the woodwork.

After prayer and counsel, we made changes to some of our financial accounts. It was really just routine maintenance; no biggie. But a few days later when we were in the middle of making breakfast, a presumptuous young emissary from an insurance company knocked on our door without an appointment and tried to insert herself into our already overloaded morning routine, and she didn't want us to make any "hasty, uninformed decisions" about our future.

She had apparently missed my last three blog posts on boundaries. But no problem; Vince gave her a crash course in less than three minutes and informed her in a few words that the only hasty decision we were making was to make her our *former* agent. We had work to do, and six hungry kiddos waiting for eggs and sausage.

Our hands were in the dirt, and people who wouldn't touch the mess with a six-foot spatula didn't hesitate to start making their general observations known. Armchair quarterbacks pitched their advice, emailing articles and suggesting books and talk show episodes. And we thought, *Those sound marvelous. If I wasn't already in the trenches, or if you could drop off a meal so I had time for a shower and a ten-minute break, I might have the luxury of attending to them. Thanks.*

We were in the middle of it, up to our elbows. This was not the time for critics in the peanut gallery to shout their questions and advice, or for Captain Obvious to express his carefully worded observations.

We weren't looking for suggestions from those with polished shoes and perfect hair. I didn't need any of the wisdom that daytime television offered. We needed comrades to partner with us, to have our back, bringing their own shovel. Or just an extra cup of coffee. We needed people with grit under their fingernails who weren't afraid of the funny smells in our house.

And the others? We waved our slimy hands at them and sent them off shrieking. We had work to do.

It was just me, behind the wheel of the Stagecoach, sitting in the parking lot, listening. I should've turned off the engine, but I was staring out the dirty window at the gravel outside and the song hadn't finished yet.

There were also – I guess I should mention this – six kids in the car with me. But they were quiet for the moment, and in just a second they would start asking if we were going in to church or not. So in this moment, in the quiet before the chaos, we just soaked. Breathed. Listened.

All day long, there were so many needs, messes, and conflicts. Why do children – or adults, for that matter – ask you a question just so they can argue with the answer you give them? I had no idea, but it drained me dry.

I was empty and needed refilling so I sat, waiting. Because I knew what would come when I paused to listen.

He would. When I showed up, He did, too.

It was nothing dramatic. No lit candles, no soft music, no clean, spacious, uncluttered floors. I was learning to listen in the middle of the mess, because waiting until after the kids were asleep was way too far away to refill when my tank was empty by lunchtime. Sometimes I coasted on fumes to the laundry room and stuck my head in the pantry, pretending to look for ingredients for dinner, and waited a few minutes right there. Sometimes Sophie came with me.

But on this day, we waited in the parking lot. The song ended and we walked into church, mismatched socks and everything. At least we all had shoes. (Some of us had sandals that showed off the mismatched socks. *So* awesome.)

We found Vince, who was already there and waiting for us. We sang, listened to announcements and a message. The tank was filling, filling...and then we worshiped again. The Holy Spirit was there the whole time, but His volume was louder now. We were singing, singing...and I knew these words of His were not for me this time. They were for the little girl standing next to me with a broken past and questionable future, and I put my right hand on top of her head.

I fought fear all the time because I knew I couldn't heal the abuse, the memories, the regression, the behavior. The only way to fight fear is with faith, which comes by hearing, even when it doesn't match what we're seeing yet. My left arm was reaching upward for more of Him because we were empty otherwise. My right hand was on her.

The song lyrics said, "You are making me new," and He said, *You are a conduit so I can fill her, too.* She needed refilling every day, also. She needed us to fight fear for her. She needed our words to speak life out of the chaos for her, so the broken past could be healed and her questions could have happy, healing answers.

November 12, 2013

A wild day for little Reagan – disobedience and resistance and holding, and she finally finished making her bed before lunchtime. She's taking a bath now; we discovered that Epsom salts are good for relaxing, detoxing, and joint pain, and I wonder if they might help with her sensory issues. Can't hurt, in any case. She has been refusing meals often since Vincent's birthday dinner – the small amount of extra attention is still more than she can handle, and people just don't understand how serious it is. But they need to know, and I'd love to not be on edge whenever we're at church or social gatherings. I hate the constant focus on negative things, but I have no idea what we'll do for the holidays this year.

I was up most of the night trying to pray, trying to picture the victory, trying to see progress, trying to decide where to go for one of the kid's eyes (which have been crossing), and trying to figure out what to do about Andrey and Reagan's attachment and development.

Then this morning I got a message from a friend. Her words were a gift:

A quick message for you today. God

wants to remind you that He has given and is continuing to give you the wisdom for each situation you face with your children. Rely on that inner voice that is Him speaking. Some of the ideas that you have been thinking seem crazy, unrelated, and impossible. I hear God saying that those ideas are His ideas for you and your family. I am praying for you today.

Twenty minutes later, she wrote again.

I was driving to another class and appointment and God began to speak again. I hope that I can adequately portray in writing the image that I saw.

I saw a little heart with string inside it. The strings connected from one side to the other, and the parts of the heart that were connected to each other didn't always make sense. As healing was brought to one place, the string would vibrate and the healing would glow to another place in this little heart.

There were some dark places in this heart where the strings were tangled and even matted. You couldn't tell one string from another. The tangles were not able to be removed; they were beyond hope. In these places of the heart I saw you reach in and gently cut away what was so damaged. As these strings were cut away, healing glowed to that dark place.

This broken and damaged heart slowly returned to health. It was like a heart of flesh. The hurt and broken places were dark spots and some were dead and rotting. As healing came, these dark places warmed to a bright red.

The heart became more and more healthy. God led and guided the hands that were bringing healing to this heart. God is leading and guiding you, Vince, and the rest of the family to bring healing to this broken heart.

I believe that you will be surprised at the work that God does in the two broken hearts that you carry. I see these hearts sitting in your hands, and your hands resting in God's hands. Slowly, bit by bit, healing flows like a small drip of oil…and at times like a huge waterfall suddenly with leaps and great speed, healing flows.

Words like this were a life raft. The Lord saw me; He saw all of us and knew. And He cared enough to interrupt friends with His words on our behalf to remind us we were not alone, and we were getting somewhere.

There's this little area of our kitchen I need to tell you about now. I'm sure your own kitchen is spotless and you've never even thought of the remote possibility of this existing in your house, but I'm referring to the tiny spaces beside the stovetop, between it and the counter – there's a little bitty crack on each side, just a millimeter or two wide. Imagine every ingredient that ever existed in our kitchen, in varying amounts from mere crumbs to several tablespoons, being forcibly crammed into it and then left to ferment. Gross.

I wiped over it daily, which was excellent for cleaning the surface around it, but probably only served to send more debris into the abyss. The only way to clean it out is to actually go in there.

Switch gears with me for a second as I tell you about another area of our house: Just a small bathroom, equipped with a light switch and perfectly good light bulbs. And in that tiny half-bath, a little girl sat on the floor, in the dark, refusing to turn on the light.

> *Children in orphanages have been conditioned to get more attention from caregivers when they appear helpless: the more independent children in an institutional environment are, the less attention they receive. Some post-institutionalized children have deeply internalized this behavior and manage to appeal to a wide audience with demonstrated helplessness.*
>
> *This behavior has also been observed in abused children, who would rather have negative reinforcement than no attention at all.*
>
> - Dr. Boris Gindis [1]

She didn't have to sit in the dark. She had everything she needed to stand up and turn on the switch and move on with her day. But it was learned helplessness combined with a medley of other attachment issues.

Trying to understand what Reagan and Andrey were doing and why they were doing it – and how we should best respond to it all in the moment – was bewildering and exhausting. Life was a cruel riddle, and I wanted answers.

Jesus! What the heck? I prayed. *Why does she do this?*

He said, *Imagine every ingredient of neglect and abuse that ever existed in the first six and a half years of her life, being forcibly crammed into her, and left to ferment. You have to go in there with her. Join her in the dark place and shine light into it.*

I opened the cracked door, and she squinted as light poured in from the hallway. I squatted down in front of her, and she flinched. She had been our daughter for over a year and still flinched when she knew she was disobeying.

It would've taken less than a second for me to flip the switch for her, and we could move on – but that would only wipe more debris into the abyss. People did that for almost seven years and clearly it did not help her, though I'm sure it seemed more convenient at the time, every time. She had to actually decide to make the move herself.

> *Many of these children actually have the needed skills or knowledge, but are resistant to any attempt to encourage them to act independently...*
>
> *It can be open defiance or hidden sabotage, but it is rooted in their overwhelming need to be always in control, to be on known and manageable "turf." This is an obstacle in their learning: to be a good learner means to take risks, to step into unknown territory, to be sure of one's own ability to cope, and to be prepared to accept help.*
>
> - Boris Gindis, Ph.D. [2]

I held her for a while and then left her to sit on the bathroom floor so I could make dinner. Spaghetti and meatballs. Homemade sauce from scratch, piece of cake.

Hey, He said. *Remember when you were in college, and didn't even know how to make coffee?*

Yeah. I couldn't make anything that didn't come out of a box or a can.

Remember when you were too intimidated to try making bread? Remember when knitting seemed too complicated? I had no idea where He was going here, but He had my attention.

Remember when you first struggled through Sense and Sensibility? *Remember when you knitted that first baby sweater? And do you remember a few months ago, when you tackled HTML and WordPress and fought until 3 am to convert the whole thing over?*

Well, yes. It took most of the weekend, but I conquered HTML and successfully converted my blog to WordPress, and felt totally victorious – that is, until the cat walked across the keyboard and completely disabled the scrolling function. It took me another hour to figure out how to fix that.

The Lord reminded me of what I'd been researching: *"To be a good learner means to take risks, to step into unknown territory, to be sure of one's own ability to cope, and to be prepared to accept help."*

You stopped being afraid of the unknown and the newness, He said. *You got tired of sitting in the dark.*

It was true. I felt like I'd spent most of my life overcoming unknowns: ridiculous anxieties, things that seemed like too much work, big and small fears, both real and nonexistent.

Yes, you have, He said. *That's why I chose you to be her mother.*

11: wild poetry

We finally achieved a major victory. Ten months earlier – or even six months earlier – I would have laughed derisively if someone had told me it could happen. But, *oh, Saturday*...we conquered you.

What used to be the day of exhaustion and mayhem every week began to behave itself with beautiful rhythm, like wild poetry. Kids cleaned their floors, made their beds, vacuumed their rooms, and you might never believe me, but some mornings there was not even a single argument.

My favorite part of this new routine was breakfast, because I no longer made it. Iree, at nine years old, took it over for me and made oatmeal every week. She loved the domestic duties of setting out bowls, putting the kettle on to boil, and chopping apples, walnuts, and pears. She did it all by herself while I leisurely drank coffee in my bathrobe and checked email with minimal disturbance.

It wasn't always perfect. There was one morning when chores were interrupted with the sound of bedroom doors slamming repeatedly, mixed with giggling. I peeked into the hallway, and heard this:

knock knock knock

"GOOD AFTERNOON," a child loudly announced, "MY NAME IS RUSSELL. I AM A JUNIOR WILDERNESS EXPLORER. ARE YOU IN NEED OF ANY ASSISTANCE TODAY, SIR?"

Another child's voice vehemently said, "NO!" and slammed the door. This scenario repeated itself until I became nervous about door hinges and put a stop to it.

But this particular morning the only interruption was a knock on my door, followed by a little mousy voice asking, "Can I have eggnog in my oatmeal?" (um, no) and a few minutes later, a request to pray so they could start eating (why, yes!). It was idyllic. I felt like I was living the dream. Not the dream I imagined, though.

My dreams are better, the Lord said. *They're out of your box.*

On my own, my box would have maybe contained a romantic ballad interspersed with some free verse. Instead, He had me in what felt like an epic allegory, seasoned with plenty of irony and the occasional salty limerick. But Saturdays were starting to be beautiful again. I still woke up earlier than I wanted, we still had chores to do, but the rhythm of the day had mellowed.

> *"But it isn't easy," said Pooh to himself... "Because Poetry and Hums aren't things which you get, they're things which get you. And all you can do is to go where they find you."*
>
> – A.A. Milne [1]

That Saturday, we finished leftover assignments from the week – a little geometry, a little writing, a chapter about Einstein, some Viking history – and then we had a nature scavenger hunt. I sent the kids out with a list of things that could be found in late fall and they came back an hour or so later with a bucket full of surprises, including but not limited to something fuzzy (moss), a dried rosehip, two kinds of seeds (one was dug out of the compost), something straight (a stick), something rough (lichen), and a chewed leaf. There was some confusion over that last item on the list, and Afton at first resigned himself to finding a dandelion leaf to chew until I clarified that it was supposed to be a leaf that a *bug* had already nibbled on. His response was an odd mixture of relief and disappointment.

We came inside and watched a knock down, drag out fight between Sophie, our older, smaller cat, and Gusser, our younger, bigger cat. (There was a clear victor at the end; it was like watching a little old lady beat the tar out of some punk with her handbag.) Then we read stories, and watched a movie, and ate popcorn with fruit for dinner. The movie was rare but the popcorn-and-fruit-for-dinner had become a weekly occurrence, and it was in this that God spoke to me again:

You need both routine and surprise, meter and free verse. They work well together – one protects your joy, and the other cultivates more of it.

But didn't we have routine and structure before, though? I asked. And we had more surprises than we wanted...so why did it take so long for...?

It takes time for the flavors to come together, He said. *It has to mellow. You have to wait for the song to come.*

Back to the school week, Chamberlain was learning to write, and the joy I felt in watching little wavery lines become faintly recognizable in those early efforts could not be expressed. She sat on the barstool across the counter while I washed dishes in the kitchen, and her preschool handwriting book was laid out in front of her. She asked me how to spell her name, and I slowly recited it for her while Sophie, indulging in one of her favorite quirks, chewed the alphabet magnets off the fridge, sending letters everywhere.

Cham held up her work to show me, and her letters were everywhere, too, all over the page. She'd taken an abstract approach to writing, completely disregarding the guide line after the word NAME that was intended to buoy it, and by sounding the letters out from left to right in order of nearest proximity, her cheerful efforts read CHMABERNAIL. Not too shabby for a four-year-old with eleven letters in her first name.

Over at the table, Afton was adding and he brought me his practice sheet. I scanned it quickly while picking up magnets Sophie had scattered all over the floor, and everything looked good except for one problem at the bottom.

"What does this say?" I asked. "Three plus six equals... backwards P?"

He grinned. "It's a *nine*..." He knew that I knew that. He also knew that I knew he could write it better.

I thought I had these guys and their older siblings figured out; we tweaked things a little every year, but overall I knew what to expect and how they should be doing in any given area.

But Andrey and Reagan were moving targets, nearly impossible to assess using any inside-the-box strategy. After teaching three kids to read by age six, teaching preschool to our eight-year-olds who were learning letters and sounds and shapes along with our four-year-old was new territory. The milestones were different, the challenges were different, and the way I had to interact with them was different than it has been with any of our other kids.

> *Writing was a trying business to Charley, who seemed to have no natural power over a pen, but in whose hand every pen appeared to become perversely animated, and to go wrong and crooked, and to stop, and splash, and sidle into corners, like a saddle-donkey.*
>
> – Charles Dickens [2]

Now we had sensory issues, institutional autism, trauma, attachment issues, fetal alcohol spectrum, and probable traumatic brain injury. Or commonly abbreviated:

SPD, IA, PTSD, RAD, FAS, and TBI. It was quite a cocktail, made more complex by the fact that some conditions are typically dealt with in ways that are counter-productive to others. For example, with attachment issues, you do ABC, and never, ever do XYZ...but with FAS, you usually do XYZ because ABC doesn't even apply. It's enough to make you want fourteen cocktails of the more traditional kind.

Teaching Andrey and Reagan in the normal way usually became a mutinous game of manipulation – if I pointed to a red circle and asked them what it was, they were just as likely to give me the wrong answer on purpose ("yellow square") as they were to give me the right answer on accident. So I learned to be sneaky with preschool, which looked like me teaching Chamberlain while Andrey and Reagan were playing nearby or looking at a book. I knew they were watching closely, listening in, but often pretending not to. And they were learning in spite of the alphabet soup of diagnoses they might be labeled with.

Sometimes they joined us to play with letters and numbers and such. But I learned to move on after just a few minutes while they were still cooperating, because if I didn't I would miss the window and manipulation would suck us into the vortex again. So we kept it short, happy, and simple, and then we changed course before it was too late.

We wrote letters on little sticky notes. We wrote letters on the windows with dry erase markers, and then covered them with the matching sticky notes. We wrote big letters in glue, and covered them with tiny pieces of torn paper to combine learning letters with sensory play and motor skills. We colored and scribbled and filled up notebooks with lines and curves that often didn't make sense.

And assessment didn't come in questions and answers – it came in the turning of the tables, when we eavesdropped on their play and conversations with each other.

risk the ocean

Did they know colors? Heck yes – just listen to them argue over Lego pieces. Could they count? Yes, they were learning to, if their games of Hide and Seek were any indication.

> *Of her childhood, Helen says herself that, save for a few impressions, "the shadows of the prison-house" enveloped it. But there were always roses, and she had the sense of smell; and there was love – but she was not loving then. When she was seven Miss Sullivan came to her. This lady had herself been blind for some years...*
>
> *It is not too much to say that imprisoned and desolate child entered upon such a large inheritance of thought and knowledge, of gladness and vision, as few of us of the seeing and hearing world attain to.*
>
> *Like all great discoveries, this, of a soul, was in all its steps marked by simplicity.*
>
> – Charlotte Mason [3]

I needed God to remind me often about why they choose to stay in the dark, and why He chose us to be their family. *This lady had herself been blind for some years...* because learning is not merely the two-way street of give and take between teacher and student. It's an ocean to navigate, and the familiar constellations were upside down in this new hemisphere, with new constellations we'd never seen before.

By this time they knew most of the letters, some numbers, and all the main colors. They knew many of the things on a preschool or kindergarten checklist...until you asked them.

I pointed to an L and put on a huge smile (because school is fun and learning letters is exciting!) and asked, "Andrey, do you know what that is?"

Andrey looked, shook his head, and put on his best pity-party frown. "I dunno."

I might've believed him, but the last two weeks had been brought to us by the letter L and we'd had it on the wall in both uppercase and lower case since September.

Well, fine. Next kid: "Reagan, what's this?"

I knew that she knew it. She knew all the letters frontwards and backwards, only occasionally stumbling over an obscure Q or W. But she just saw what Andrey did, and she was going to try it, too.

Blank stare. "I dunno," she said.

In a heroic effort I refrained from violently and repeatedly slamming my head into the nearest wall. Instead, I moved on to Chamberlain. And they didn't know it, but I wasn't teaching letters anymore.

"Cham, what's this?"

"An L." *Duh, Mom.*

"Great job! Hey...which sticker do you want?" *Because learning letters is exciting!*

The I Dunno's blank expressions quickly changed. That was not the reaction they were expecting – learned helplessness is usually met with extra attention, not indifference. But now they were learning that those coveted stickers come to those who are honest.

It felt like a win for that day, but it never felt like enough. Reagan would be eight soon, and some days it seemed like we were getting the loose ends tied together only to have them cut apart with scissors the next time we went out in public.

They should be learning shapes. We should paint more often. I should read more intentionally to them. I should teach them more about animals. I should email that per-

son about the occupational therapist they mentioned. I should go to sleep before 2 am.

Those letters – the ones that spell *should* – went everywhere.

Sophie pulled the magnets and artwork off the fridge again and I rearranged them higher, out of her reach, as I thought about what I should be doing better. Between cooking and bathing and laundry and cleaning, it never felt like enough. The day was spent in knitting little hearts together, and by bedtime everything felt unraveled.

Just feed them and love them, the Holy Spirit said. *They are learning and healing in that. It is enough.*

When you feel like it's not, that's only because you are completely disregarding the guideline that was intended to buoy you.

In my own way, I knew I was making a lot of backwards Ps that were supposed to be nines, too.

Each day is an enduring triumph, accomplishing My purpose, He said. *The work of your day is everlasting, steadfastly working out the calling I've set out for it. It's not fraying or unraveling tomorrow, like dishes that will need to be washed again after the next meal.*

I know you're learning. Your letters go everywhere because you are actually trying. I'm watching your efforts with joy the same way you watch Chamberlain write. I can't express to you the joy I feel in watching your lines become recognizable in these early efforts.

The woods were a dull, soft brown that snowless November, and our kids were totally confused about what season it was. It wasn't really fall anymore because the leaves were long gone, but it couldn't be winter yet because there was still no snow. Instead we had green grass in our yard that reached its full height of about two inches and then stalled, refusing to grow more.

Green grass does not belong in the November picture at all. It's completely out of place, like so many other things in our house: cheap plastic tops tucked in bookshelf décor, pink froggy tub toys next to my African violets on the windowsill, a green wooden alligator on top of vintage copies of Plutarch and Cicero.

That season, that year, was an entirely different critter. We woke up one morning to frost that neutralized color on everything it touched, so we knew winter was coming soon. The odd, extended fall with its steaming chai tea, flannel shirts, and diminishing daylight was about to give way to 4pm sunsets, extra down comforters, and 10 degrees below zero soon enough.

```
November 19, 2013

Bitterly cold here, minus ten, and the
crock pot has been going all day with
potato stew. I have two kids soaking in
Epsom salt baths, two little girls getting
jammies on, and two boys downstairs prac-
ticing Spanish so they can earn video game
time. When put that way, it sounds like I
know what I'm doing around here.
```

Reagan's second birthday with us arrived, and I wrote her a letter that she will probably never be able to read. But it was healing for me.

Dear Reagan,

You turned eight years old today. You had little idea what it meant, and you didn't know what you wanted for cake or presents. You knew you got extra hugs and smiles today.

You came to us full of fear and hurts and hunger and unknowns. I would lean in, you would lean away. You were wary, untrusting, hesitant. You were afraid of stairs, of animals, of not being fed. You panicked at the smell of food that was not right in front of you. You were afraid of us, especially of me. You walked with a lurch and flapped your arms when you were excited. You still flap a little, but so much less.

You can wait for food now. You know it will come to you as soon as it's ready.

You play now. You love to play with buttons and cars, and you look at books quietly on the couch every day. You especially like cookbooks.

Now you can run. You dress yourself, you make your bed, you fold clothes, and you even refuse food to push us away sometimes – but at least that means that you aren't afraid of starving anymore.

You used to be hot and cold, swinging from one extreme to the other in your affection and rejection of us. You would cling aggressively one day, and shove us away the next. Now you are...well, definitely not lukewarm. You've leveled out to warm and cool. It's progress, and we'll take it.

You are learning to speak. You are learning to give and maintain eye contact to those who love you. You are learning letters, colors, and shapes, and you can count to eight. You know how much four is. You know that you were seven yesterday, and now you are eight. Whatever that means.

But you don't know that we prayed for you when you were a toddler. I'm so sorry it took us so long to find you. You don't know that we saw you, found you, and chose you when you were five. That we waited and prayed and cried for you until we got to meet you when you were six, and that we brought you home months later when you were pushing seven.

You probably don't know very much about the years before that. We don't, either.

We have a few pictures of you as a toddler, but they are undated and we can only guess how old you were in them. We have paperwork that mentions inaccurate diagnoses that are both more and less severe than the truth of what you are healing through. It says you didn't learn to walk until you were almost three years old.

You almost never flinch anymore when I reach toward you. In the middle of the night, when you're asleep and I tuck you in one more time before I go to bed, your arm doesn't fly up in fear anymore to cover your face. I'm so sorry you ever had to do that, and that you ever felt like you had to do that here.

You are healing. You are growing and learning and we are seeing more and more of the real you, and you shine. You are brave. You are strong. You are gentle and curious and tender and joyful. You are growing in wisdom and stature, just as the One who redeemed you did when He was young.

You have a mighty future. We are so honored to be in it.

With a love that grows and prays for your mountains to move,

Mama

12: just keep it together

We spent that Thanksgiving alone. Extended family members had their own lives and events, and the normal annual gathering didn't seem like a good idea with our new situation. Some people understood, but others didn't, and I grieved the changes I couldn't control.

Letting go of control was not an overnight process for me; my conversion from Type A to Type B was still in the highly experimental beta stage. I was making progress; for example, I broke up with Martha Stewart. Her photos were gorgeous, her style was impressive, but meals categorized as "quick and simple dinners" should require less than nineteen steps, two food processors, and a therapist.

Our third post-adoption home visit was approaching and I knew the social worker would ask the same big, impossible question that everyone else did: *How are you doing?* There was never a simple answer; it was up and down, forward and backward. We measured progress in micro-steps, and the manipulation and disobedience bordered on levels of insanity.

By now we'd learned that both Andrey and Reagan were terrified of (and resistant to) many forms of success, celebration, and achievement, and often regressed instantly and violently after any victory. We discovered this was common among kids with similar backgrounds of trauma, neglect, and abandonment – extremely common among kids who grew up in orphanages – but it made things like school, potty training, holidays, and, you know, waking hours difficult.

Including birthdays. Andrey's second birthday with us rolled around, and we had a few presents wrapped and a low-key dinner planned. Just us, nothing disruptive. But it was no bueno; misbehavior followed misbehavior, poor choices compounded, and he sabotaged his special day at every opportunity to turn it around. We offered love, belonging, fun times, and he refused it all, like refusing chocolate only to go back to maggoty gruel. His birthday should have been so fun; we wanted to celebrate his life with him, and watching him refuse it was heartbreaking.

People raised their eyebrows when we explained the level of trauma Andrey and Reagan came from and the boundaries we had to place because of it. I hated it when people asked, "You're still dealing with that?" because it felt like it was our fault. Other people's expectations were unfair, but mine were no better. I thought that surely Andrey and Reagan would be delightfully law abiding citizens after being in a loving home for eighteen months, despite the fact that they were neglected and abused for almost seven years.

And I had to say it in as loving a manner as I could muster: *Friends and family, please don't rush us.* Man, we wanted this way more than anyone else did. We hoped it would be easier. Of course we hoped attachment wouldn't be an issue. We knew it was likely, though.

There's this annoying little theory out there that says for every year your adopted child was in an institution, that is how many years it may take him or her to heal. And no promises, even with that. So I did the math, and thought, *By then, Vincent will be eighteen. He might be moving out of the house by the time our house feels normal again.* This is part of what we signed up for.

And then I thought about bingeing on ice cream and moving to a convent and how bad it hurts when mascara gets in your eyes when you're sobbing. I thought of other things not fit to print. And also how I'm married, and not Catholic, and the nuns probably wouldn't take me anyway.

And I thought of how God must feel when He offers a new beginning and we reject Him over and over. The book of Hosea was all too real to us now; we knew what it was to love and to be shunned, to pray and cry and offer redemption to people who persisted in choices that hurt them and us.

> *Yet it was I who taught Ephraim to walk; I took them up by their arms, but they did not know that I healed them. I led them with cords of kindness, with the bands of love, and I became to them as one who eases the yoke on their jaws, and I bent down to them and fed them.*
>
> *– Hosea 11:3-4*

Our kids were hurting, and we were often hurting, too. Adoption always starts with grief. They coped with the chaos of their early years by creating chaos around them. Ready or not, adoptive parents choose to live it out with them, and the biological kids have to come along for the ride.

And living it out is often a lonely journey. In spite of how common that loneliness is, few people talk about it and that makes it even lonelier. But adoptive parents have good reasons for staying quiet: We don't want to dissuade everyone from adoption. We don't want to share embarrassing details about our kids' behavior, or private information about their history. We don't want to be judged by the ignorant. And we don't want advice from armchair quarterbacks who confuse watching an episode of a talk show with actual experience in early childhood psychology and attachment disorder.

We want to be *nice*. Usually.

We also want our kids to take the chocolate we offer them – love, belonging, fun times – and stop going back to the maggoty gruel they are familiar with. We want them to seek out and enjoy victory, instead of shooting themselves in the foot and sabotaging their success. We want them to be the same people at home as they are in public. We want the quick insta-grin they give the camera in the midst of a sulking fit to actually be a genuine smile, instead of a charming mask that covers anxiety and anger. We want it to happen before they turn eighteen. And before our other kids turn eighteen, too.

But we had no regimented minute-by-minute agendas to achieve that. Just a loose schedule with firm standards, attempting to run a tight ship in choppy waters.

```
January 31, 2014

It's 1:30am. I just checked on the kiddos
to tuck them all in again – Vincent and
Afton asleep, Andrey pretending to be,
though I can tell he isn't because he's
sucking his thumb. When I kissed him, I
whispered, "Don't suck your thumb, Andrey,"
and he said "Okay," totally alert. He had a
great, amazing day. I'm wary and watchful
but praising God for it.
The girls were all asleep. Cham had tummy
issues today and I covered her again and
kissed her, and just kept my hand on her
back, so thankful for that tiny, precious,
hilarious, beautiful one who attests to
healthy attachment and great joy. I turned
to Reagan and covered her again (she always
throws the blankets off) and I thought of
```

how she never had a mommy to pat her back until now, and even once she was home, she was afraid of being disturbed at night. She almost never acts that way anymore, though she, too, pretends to be asleep when I kiss her goodnight before I go to bed. She told me today, "You no mama!" and it's a new milestone I wasn't looking forward to.

I learned today that someone found my blog by googling "Bulgaria adoption, throw fit in grocery store." For the record, our kids lean more toward throwing fits in the privacy of our home after guests leave, with the rare exception of large holiday gatherings at the Sports Complex. So there.

In other news, two sets of our close friends are moving out of state. We expected it from one of them, didn't see it coming with the other. I'm trying not to feel anything.

A child came up to me, took my hand, and brought me to the living room. She wanted to show me what she'd been playing with. This by itself wasn't remarkable. What was remarkable was it was Reagan, and she was showing her own imaginative play, all by herself, for the first time — not just going along with someone else's idea, but making up her own story. Not copying a familiar scenario, but coming up with something totally on her own. We had never seen her do that before, and have rarely seen her do it since.

She pointed to a baby doll, wrapped in a messy blanket on the couch.

"Oh, mama. See baby…"

I looked at the baby, and I looked at her.

"Oh, mama…oh, baby…baby ick at de puh ook mama!"

Right, I had no idea what she said, either.

"Baby ick, mama! Baby seep on cowse, baby pook!" She vividly illustrated with a gagging sound, repeated the phrase, and then burst out laughing.

Ah. *Baby asleep on couch, baby puke.* Gotcha.

"Oh! Baby's sick? Baby puked?" I asked.

Enthusiastic nodding. "Oh, poor baby..." she said, totally grinning.

"Aww, should we pray for the baby?"

She raised her eyebrows in an are-you-serious kind of look. Still grinning, though.

"Dear Jesus — Reagan, put your hand on the baby — please heal Baby and help her sleep and not puke anymore." She laughed outright, as if it's okay for her to pretend a doll is sick, but totally nuts for me to pretend to pray for it. Giggles erupted, overflowing.

She was still concerned about food, but not usually in the panicking, freaky-outy kind of way anymore, just a slightly anxious and very curious way. So as I made dinner she started asking questions.

"Eskoose me, Mama? You make bockbock?"

"Nope, not popcorn..."

"You make soup?"

"Yep..."

"An den you make...*biscuit*?!"

"No biscuits tonight, sorry."

But in my head I was screaming, *You said "and then!" You are thinking about a logical sequence of events, and grouping things together! You know that soup usually goes with biscuits! Awesome!* This was the same week she took on sledding all by herself, hauling her sled across the ice and up the bunny hill behind our house, over and over again, and loving it.

Just stir the soup and keep it together, Mama. Sheesh.

We'd fought fear that she would never do these things. We still fight, really. Will our kids ever be able to do the things they are supposed to do? Will they ever stop doing the things they're *not* supposed to do? Will we ever catch up, slow down, meet deadlines, remember appointments, and achieve milestones?

At one in the morning, praying in the shower, I was totally exhausted, emptied, and discouraged after a day of herding uncooperative minions. It all intensified into one question: *What do I do?* Maybe the battle you fight looks different, but we both know what it is to be under fire, overwhelmed, and out of answers. You, me, the whole mess of us.

> *And He who searches hearts knows what is the mind of the Spirit, because the Spirit intercedes for the saints according to the will of God.*
>
> – Romans 8:27

Oh, God...what do I do? My biggest concerns never fit on my to-do list for the next day. The cease-fire would end in less than eight hours, and I was running out of hot water.

> *Who is to condemn? Christ Jesus is the one who died—more than that, who was raised—who is at the right hand of God, who indeed is interceding for us.*
>
> – Romans 8:34

Trust Me, He said. *You've never seen Me do this before.*

He reminded me to lay low, refusing to be provoked, while the chaos drifted overhead, a bully looking for a reaction. The person who falls for it is a reckless shooter who rarely hits the right target, and usually only creates more victims. There are enough angry people out there, bleeding insecurity in the form of rash arrogance.

You have My permission to take it slow. To aim before you fire. Just one thing at a time, and let Me handle the big picture. Watch and listen for it, Love, while you reload. You just wait.

The volume didn't necessarily change, but a calm settled.

Your babies have been sick, but I'm praying for them.

> *Consequently, he is able to save to the uttermost those who draw near to God through him, since he always lives to make intercession for them.*
>
> *– Hebrews 7:25*

I'm not copying an old scenario that you've seen before, He said. *I'm making a whole new story.*

```
March 5, 2014

Close friends of ours have brought their
adopted son home. And I know it's just the
beginning, and I'm thrilled for them, and
of course I hope it continues wonderful-
ly...but when he tells them he loves them
after only a few days and we've never heard
that from either of our kids eighteen
months into this, it's hard. It is selfish-
ly, whiningly, self-pityingly painful to
watch the sunshine and roses elsewhere.
I am so tired, and tomorrow is another
day. When most people say that, it's sup-
posed to be infused with hope and promise,
but tomorrow just seems like the threat of
having to relive all the miseries and
hassles of today. And I'd rather not...so I
guess I should pray.
I read this quote today:
```

> *It is a law of our nature with which it is absolutely useless to contend, and our only means of true intimacy with a child is the power of recovering our own childhood – a power which we are apt to let slip as of no vital importance.*
>
> *– Charlotte Mason* [1]

Apparently it's common enough that the experience has a name: parallel healing. So much of the healing of their childhood demands me to address the healing still required from my own. And I'm burned out on discipline, homeschooling, chores, cooking, defying, bickering, disobeying...but actually, it's been a pretty good week.

It's not that I don't believe anymore that my greatest work and influence in this time is in raising these kids. It is; I still believe that. It is that I feel like I'm not doing it as well when it's *all* I'm doing, *all* of the time. My effort, joy, and passion are diluted from giving all my time to it, and not much is left. I feel like anything I give to another area – writing, especially – steals from my parenting, when really those areas give to each other. I constantly fight mom guilt and inadequacy.

In the middle of a word, the point of my pen broke and tore right through the paper. It was my favorite pen – just a cheap one, but it had the perfect grip, the right color, and the enchanting ability to make spider scrawl legible. Despite the miles of perfectly wonderful writing left in it, it was rendered useless because the tip broke off and left it so sharp that it bled ink and ripped everything it touched.

Probably because I'm stubborn (whatever), I was determined to resurrect it with salvaged parts from an expendable pen. It ended up taking one patient husband and three pairs of pliers, but fifteen minutes later the pen was back in action. My fingers were covered in dark blue splotches, and I thought, *Oh...Jo would be proud.*

We'd been reading *Little Women*, all of us, aloud on the weekends. On a peaceful, Sunday evening, you would find us all crowded on the couch, but don't imagine anything too idealistic. When we got to the part where Beth was sick, and Jo says, "Oh, my precious—" she was interrupted by two of our children eerily gasping out in unison, *"My preciousss!!"* and the mood was broken, just like that.

When we were six hundred pages into the book, Vince handed it to me when we got to that certain chapter. You know the one. And I was fine – amazed myself, really – until I read to:

> *So the spring days came and went, the sky grew clearer, the earth greener, the flowers were up fair and early, and the birds came back in time to say goodbye –* [2]

– and my voice escaped me. Nothing would come out, and I handed to book back to Vince.

Afton looked back and forth at us. "Time to put the book in the freezer?" He was eight at the time, and I swear he's never seen an episode of "Friends" in his life.

We made it, though. Vince and I took turns through that part, as we did with a lot of things in that season. I felt completely walled in from never leaving the house and never talking in person to adults except for an hour on Sundays. Like my pen, I was dark blue, sharp, and feeling overused. My top blew off and I realized I'd been bleeding on my kids, who were starting to tear into each other.

> *Poor Jo! These were dark days for her, for something like despair came over her when she thought of spending all her life in that quiet house, devoted to humdrum cares, a few poor little pleasures, and the duty that never seemed to grow any easier. "I can't do it. I wasn't meant for a life like this, and I know I shall break away and do something desperate if somebody don't come and help me," she said to herself, when her first efforts failed, and she fell into the moody, miserable state of mind which often comes when strong wills have to yield to the inevitable.*

– Louisa May Alcott [3]

Aside from church, I hadn't been out of the house in weeks. I hadn't left the house on my own in months. And, reclusive homebody or not, I needed to breathe. I wasn't meant for a life like this.

> *The objects which bore us, or the persons who bore us, appear to wear a bald place in the mind, and thought turns from them with sick aversion.*

– Charlotte Mason [4]

We took drastic measures, though they probably sound silly to you. For three days in a row, Vin sent me out of the house.

I went to the library by myself and browsed every section without a single interruption. I went to an appointment and to the post office. Once, I ran errands with only half of our kids – the three who weren't busted for lying that day – and I experienced the perspective that comes when you discover that what used to be overwhelming is now quiet relief.

I started to remember what these days are meant for.

And then I met one of my best friends for coffee. She was getting ready to move, and we talked deeply about our past, our present, and our plans for the future, including at least one facetiously arranged marriage between our children. In those three hours we cried about eleven times, but I drove home almost fully resuscitated.

> *Meaninglessness inhibits fullness of life and is therefore equivalent to illness. Meaning makes a great many things endurable – perhaps everything...*
>
> – Carl Jung

The ho-hum and the agony diminished in the fresh air and I came home ready to finish this chapter, determined not to be rendered useless from a little breaking. Miles of perfectly good ink were left in us, and we were meant for this. Vin and I worked so well together because he's a patient husband...and because I'm stubborn, probably.

13: a path which few can tell


```
April 9, 2014

Feeling overwhelmed. Paperwork and writ-
ing deadlines, one of the cats has been
sick, and I'm rewarding all non-whiners
with chocolate today. Not sure if this
makes me the coolest mom ever, or the most
desperate.
```

It was snowing outside and a child screamed, "I want my hat! I want my hat!" on repeat at our back door. I could only imagine what the neighbors might think, and prayed they weren't home. If they were, they would see a small boy, about four years old, raging on the back deck with his jacket, shoes, and one mitten...but no hat.

They wouldn't see the backstory, though, which was that the boy was actually eight years old and had refused his hat after being disobedient all morning, stomping and disruptive everywhere, and was sent outside to do some therapeutic jumping on the rebounder to help him reset and give the rest of us a little peace.

"You have two minutes to get what you need," I told him, and set the timer. He used that time to scream and rampage while his oldest brother watched from the workbench, tinkering with a project.

The timer went off and I mustered a chipper, "It's time to go out now...take your time and work out all those feelings while you jump." Smile, with kind eyes, as he growled in my face on his way out the door. Inwardly I was shaking, taking deep breaths, trying to get enough oxygen to calm my racing thoughts.

```
June 2, 2014

   Sophie had another seizure today. Her
body twisted and trembled and she seemed
alert the whole time; she couldn't get her
legs to cooperate with her spine and her
brain. But she's moving more tonight, more
than she did after that first episode a
couple months ago. I'm fighting so much
fear. I need light, and hope, and joy.
Jesus.


June 6, 2014

   I think if all the kids would just a)
speak clearly, and b) stop putting poop in
the wrong places on purpose, we might real-
ly win this thing. We've caught one of them
twice painting fecal matter on the walls,
toilets, and mirrors.


June 13, 2014

   I am better, but only if I'm trying to be
prophetic or dishonest. Sophie's had a hard
time walking for the last several days, two
of our kids are at odds and increasing the
discord, and one of my best friends leaves
the state in a few days. I'm at a loss, and
so fearful about Sophie. God help us.
```

June 14, 2014

She was in the corner, not moving, so I put her on my lap. She's so soft that touching her is a gift, but I'm afraid to hurt her. She's been such a comfort to me; I don't want to be a discomfort to her.

I swing between resignation and despondent urgency, begging for her healing. My left hand is on her as I type one-handed – that trick I learned while nursing the last baby – and she's on a bath towel because she couldn't make it to the bathroom last time and I found her in a puddle, urine soaking into her white fur. She keeps trying to hide, but it's like she has no idea where she's going.

This is a nauseating grief, partly because it must sound so trivial in light of everything else, as though I shouldn't grieve like this for a pet. But she's more than that. She's older than our first child, and she's the one who's with me, waking and sleeping, more than anyone else in the family.

Every patch of light looked like her out of the corner of my eye – a pillow, a blanket, a sunbeam. The pain of losing this companion devastated with every reminder of her absence. She wasn't sleeping on the couch, wasn't laying on the laundry, wasn't loitering in the bathroom every time someone wanted to use it.

I just could not believe her to be gone after she had been so present in my every moment. After Vin went to work, she was with me. After everyone was asleep and I was the only one still awake, I was praying and she was with me. She'd always been with me. She became one of my closest friends – which wasn't an insult to the human friends in our lives, but just how uncommonly wonderful she was. I woke up at night and prayed through anxiety, and she was right there next to me. I'd come upstairs for a breather at intervals throughout the day, and she was next to my writing table. After I tucked the kids into bed she curled up on my lap, and while I read the Bible, she was with me.

One of my best friends – the one who moved away the day after Sophie died, and I faced the days ahead without either of them – reassured me that none of this was weird or silly or trivial. She said some people have prayer shawls, but I had had a prayer cat. It made perfect sense.

Sophie had been breathing deeply on the evening of Father's Day, her face tucked into a corner between my Bible and the flannel she'd been sleeping on. She'd suddenly lost her vision, walking in circles, bumping into things. Sleeping with her eyes partly open. I just watched her breathe – her side rising and falling, as she slept facing the window. I picked up white clouds of fur from her staggered wanderings the night before.

Sometimes she pawed her front legs like she was kneading something, and if I touched her paw she gripped my finger and stopped, while the other paw kept seeking.

I put on worship music and read the Psalms – this was no time for Leviticus, where my bookmark was. I had other books to read also, but none of them were a part of this time, right here, in the closeness of the pain and quiet. I had laundry to do and clothes to change, but I didn't want to miss her leaving.

We prepared the kids at bedtime and cried with them, answering questions, explaining as much as we could. We prayed, tucked them in, and checked on her. And she was still pawing, but with all four legs now, like she was picking up speed, running to the Lion who loves her.

We went back downstairs to the couch, and Vin and I prayed. She was usually there with us every night, and we talked about all the little things we missed her doing – waiting for us on the stairs when we pulled in the driveway, tearing the magnets and kids' artwork off the fridge, sleeping shamelessly on the warm counter when the dishwasher was running underneath it.

> *And as He spoke, He no longer looked to them like a lion; but the things that began to happen after that were so great and beautiful that I cannot write them.*
>
> *And for us this is the end of all the stories, and we can most truly say that they all lived happily ever after. But for them it was only the beginning of the real story.*
>
> *All their life in this world and all their adventures in Narnia had only been the cover and the title page: now at last they were beginning Chapter One of the Great Story which no one on earth has read: which goes on forever: in which every chapter is better than the one before.*
>
> – C.S. Lewis [1]

We finished praying, and went back upstairs to check on her. And she was warm, but just gone...caught up with the Lion who loves her, and us.

I was surrounded by chocolates. Or, to be honest, I was surrounded by a variety of wrappers and a few leftover chocolates that barely escaped with their lives. We pitched up and down the waves, rocking and weeping until the wee hours.

> *If you've been up all night and cried till you have no more tears left in you – you will know that there comes in the end a sort of quietness. You feel as if nothing was ever going to happen again.*
>
> -C.S. Lewis [2]

That eerie calm settles on the heels of grief, and when the hits keep coming we look at the future and wonder if this is a pattern we need to just face with bleak resignation. *My cat is gone. My friend is gone. My life as I knew it has been long gone, and I don't like the way this is heading.*

I was reading the book of John and got to the part about Martha and Mary and the raising of Lazarus. And He caught me on that one little verse and kept me there: Jesus wept.

Why, though? He knew He was going to raise Lazarus in just a few minutes. If He knew it was going to be good, why did He give in to grief in the meantime?

I think it has to do with what Martha said to Him a little earlier: "Lord, if you had been here, my brother would not have died." And a few minutes later, Mary came and said the same thing.

> *Now when Mary came to where Jesus was and saw Him, she fell at His feet, saying to Him, "Lord, if you had been here, my brother would not have died."*
>
> – John 11:32

They knew it, and He knew it. And I knew it, too. It was this: *You could have prevented this.*

In every loss we experience, it's true. We're aching and heaving, and He could have prevented it. Sometimes He does, more than we realize. And sometimes He doesn't. And He weeps and rocks with us...more than we realize.

> *When Jesus saw her weeping, and the Jews who had come with her also weeping, He was deeply moved in His spirit and greatly troubled.*
>
> – John 11:33

Then He does something else that seems odd.

> *And He said, "Where have you laid him?" They said to Him, "Lord, come and see."*
>
> – John 11:34

Where did they *lay* him? Why did He ask that? Didn't Jesus, the God-man, already know? It was more than that, though. He wasn't just asking where the dead man was.

He was saying, *Show me where it hurts.*

And that's when He cried.

He weeps with Mary and Martha – and us – because He understands that sometimes we experience loss and pain for the sake of the expansion of the Kingdom. He knows we come under attack and we don't know how to handle all the upheaval. He weeps with us because He knows we hurt and we often don't understand why. He knows we rock in agony with no answers; He knows our ship swings between the violence and the lullaby.

In loss – whether it's the death of a person, a pet, our plans, or something else entirely – we want certainty and explanation, but what we usually get first is refinement. We learn a little more about what it is to walk into the unknown, blank pages He sends us into. Please don't misunderstand me; I'm not talking about accepting a hindrance, sickness, or other harassment from the enemy. We must not fall for his trick of casting righteous-sounding blame on God for attacks that come from the pit of hell. Denying ourselves and following Him is a mission, not a malady. The calling out of our comfort zone is our cross.

Sometimes, because He causes all things for good for those who love Him, grief and loss launch us farther and faster into His assignment for us. He knows it's hard and it grieves Him, too. But He also knows what's coming.

> *Jesus said to her, "Did I not tell you that if you believed you would see the glory of God?"*
>
> *– John 11:40*

We learn not to love our life so much – not because we're ungrateful or bitter, but because we are unfettered and surrendered. We know this place isn't permanent.

We're not resigned. We're reloading. And He's not taking our life; He's resurrecting it.

Our girl said, "I ya you, mama," and I wasn't sure if she meant it, or if she even knew what it meant yet, but she had heard it over and over from us and finally felt safe to say it back. It had taken two years.

And him...he waved, all smiles. I gave him a thumbs up, and he gave a thumbs up back, instead of the equivalent to the middle finger, which is what we were used to. He also went through a phase of saying "I love you" and it was heart-meltingly sweet at first, but then we realized that aggressive or defiant behavior followed it every time.

So there was progress, but we were hard to please because we wanted it to be faster than two steps forward, 1.9 steps back. We were past the stage of not recognizing our home anymore, but not yet to the point of getting to go out of the house for dates yet. I had vague memories about our life before adoption, including certain things that made it possible for us to leave the house without children – I think they were called "babysitters?" – but they were as extinct as the dodo.

But most days we saw light at the end of the tunnel and we were pretty confident that it wasn't an oncoming freight train. I was reading about mythical heroes to the kids, and we came across the life of Perseus:

> *So Perseus started on his journey...till he came to the Unshapen Land, and the place which has no name.*
>
> *And seven days he walked through it, on a path which few can tell; for those who go there again in dreams are glad enough when they awake; till he came to the edge of the everlasting night, where the air was full of feathers, and the soil was hard with ice; and there at last he found the three Gray Sisters, by the shore of the freezing sea, nodding upon a white log of drift-wood, beneath the cold white winter moon; and they chanted a low song together, "Why the old times were better than the new."*
>
> *There was no living thing around them, not a fly, not a moss upon the rocks.*
>
> – Charles Kingsley [3]

And I was no hero, but this journey often felt like the place which has no name. I often sang the same song.

Another adoptive mom wrote me this:

> *I told my husband just yesterday, "Adoption is the loneliest thing you will ever do," and I wondered out loud why would God call people to adopt if it only leaves them feeling alone and isolated....an island in a world that pays little attention...and he said, "It is not God's will that we are alone...it is a heart condition of our society."*

I agree with both of them. I don't think it's an intentional heart condition, but an undiagnosed heart condition, made possible by the combination of media misinformation and a shallow culture that is content to believe it, because those who get their hands dirty threaten to mess up the manicures of the comfortable.

> *If we are afflicted, it is for your comfort and salvation; and if we are comforted, it is for your comfort, which you experience when you patiently endure the same sufferings that we suffer. Our hope for you is unshaken, for we know that as you share in our sufferings, you will also share in our comfort.*
>
> *– 2 Corinthians 1:6-7*

But friends, post-adoption depression is real, and common, and serious. It's a different beast than postpartum or any other depression, and it comes with a myriad of its own mutilated griefs, but they're all spawn of the same ugly monster.

Life doesn't go on hold for families who bring hurting children into their homes, and in many cases like ours, they deal with drama and attack from several directions outside the home as well. If you know an adoptive or foster family, or a special needs family, or a family who falls into both categories (and many do), for the love of all that is holy, pray for them. The Unshapen Land isn't a place we linger or stay, but it has lessons to teach for those who trod the bleak path there. Your prayer helps them come out wiser and well-armed, so they can slay the monster and finish the task before them.

14: teamwork

I wonder if, as they all grow to adulthood, my kids will look back and remember that their mama sang hymns when they were little. And also, I wonder if they will ever realize that many of those quietly sung hymns happened to coincide with their temper tantrums and outbursts, and that the repeated humming chorus of "It is Well With My Soul" might have been the only thing that kept them from completely frying her grits, and kept her from committing a felony.

We had our last post-adoption placement meeting in late June. We were done, *finis*, stick a fork in us, no more paperwork or meetings. And it was fine, really; only one small hiccup when we were conversing on the lawn with the social worker, and Vince caught Afton bringing an eight-foot birch pike out of the woods.

Alarmed, Vin nonchalantly moved toward him and quietly whispered, "Afton, no pike battles while the social worker is here."

Afton immediately turned around – so far, so good – and shouted to his brother.

"Hey! Dad says we can't have a pike battle *till she leaves!*" So close. Thanks, buddy.

Summer came in full force with other unwelcome visitors, and we discovered that if a mosquito wakes you up around 3:00 a.m. by buzzing your ear, it's possible to smash it into the side of your head with such violence in your groggy stupor that it not only kills the mosquito but also knocks you out cold. (It's also possible that you won't hear any more mosquitoes for the next several nights...out of *that* ear, at least.)

The front yard contained a gigantic blue-tarp-turned-kiddie-pool, a rigged zipline, and often, a boy forty feet up a spruce tree. That was the summer almost all of our kids learned to whistle with grass blades (my most sincere apologies to the entire Mat-Su Borough) and it felt like I was in an episode of Duck Dynasty, and either needed an intervention or a trucker hat.

But what I really wanted was a pair of kittens.

I began haunting the classifieds and threatened that if we didn't bring some home soon, I was going to paint whiskers on Chamberlain. Fortunately for her (though I don't think she would've minded) we found five-week-old littermates who had been abandoned by their barn cat mama. We named the buff tabby Bingley and his tiny black sister Knightley, and their arrival brought a shift to the atmosphere in our home.

In the mornings when I bent over the sink to wash my face, twenty tiny needles would suddenly impale my left leg, and then start climbing. I'd grab the towel to dry off with one hand while blindly grasping for the ascending kitten with the other hand. But it takes a while to disentangle twenty tiny claws even when you're not blinking water out of your eyes, and before I had it done, kapow, twenty more needles started climbing my other pant leg. They took turns evading my grasp and scaling my jeans before I escaped, gasping for air, to shut the little sinners in the bathroom behind me.

But then they slept and snuggled, and it was just bliss...for most of us, at least. We made a song about it; it goes "*Gusser and the kittens, and then there were three: H-I-S-S-I-N-G.*" Our other cat, like many older siblings, didn't know what to make of these tiny intruders and he wasn't sure how to defend himself against them without getting in trouble. And like many younger siblings, the kittens were fearless, immune to intimidation, and had no sense of personal space. Gus could growl, spit, bully, and use all sorts of feline profanity and they still approached him with wide-eyed adoration. *Hey, wanna be friends? Do you wanna play? Do you wanna build a snowman? No? Okay, maybe later! I'm gonna go poop in your litterbox now, yay!!*

And here's a weird thing: I felt *so* guilty for adoring and bonding with the kittens. They constantly scratched, bit, and created chaos in their wake – so, why were the kittens funny and cute, while broken children who instigated destruction and mayhem were so aggravating and heartbreaking? Both were innocent in some measure, motivated by instinct and survival. On one side, I felt faithless and hypocritical. But on the other side, I remember laughing again…and realizing that I hadn't laughed in months. Maybe longer.

Now I understand a little of what happened: I had known what to expect from kittens, and their snuggles covered a multitude of sins. But I hadn't known what to expect from Andrey and Reagan, and what did come was so much harder than I'd anticipated. Plus, any affection they gave that might have made up for it was rare and disingenuous. The kittens' presence didn't turn our home upside down or demand permanent and painful changes to our lifestyle. But my heart didn't understand that it was an unfair correlation. Contrasting kittens with adopted, special needs children wasn't even comparing apples to oranges; it was comparing apples to a gigantic basket of various fruits, some of which had been injected with toxins.

Andrey and Reagan were healing, too, but it was like exploratory surgery without anesthesia. We all could've lived without the surgery but it would have been less like living later on: We would've been drawn to God's heart and each other less, and His call on our lives would've felt less imperative as we learned to ignore it and numb ourselves to His voice. The covering of His protection as we obeyed may not have been there, exposing us to any number of unknown terrors He sheltered us from unawares.

But among kids and kittens, we had enough rivalry, tattling, criticism, arguing, scratching, snatching, and hissing to make any mom beg for a dose of anesthesia. The big ones picked on the little ones. The little ones provoked and pestered the big ones. And we parents wondered where we missed the mark.

We were trying to teach our kids to be encouragers instead of critics and to get the plank out of their own eyes and mind their own business. It's hard to model this as a mom because, well, I was bossing them about not bossing each other ("I'm *not* bossing him, I'm *telling* him!" a child said once) and after years of parenting, I was still learning to step back and wait before intervening, and just let them take it outside and have at each other...I mean, problem solve and work through conflict. Yeah, that's it.

Sometimes it worked out pretty well:

> Cham: I'm little. I'm five.
> Andrey: Vincent's big. He's nine.
> Cham: No, he's thirteen. He's the biggest.
> Andrey: Well, I'm little, too. I'm five.
> Cham: No, you're big. You're eight.
> Andrey: I'm *eight*?! (I thought for sure he had that figured out by now.)

Other times, we learned that a surprising amount of controversy can come from something as innocent as a peaceful, ten-minute drive spent looking at Christmas lights because while the older kids counted up how many they saw, the little kids randomly yelled out big numbers to help, like "Thirty-eight! Nineteen-two! Twenty-leven!" and comments ensued that threatened to move everyone to Santa's naughty list.

And every once in a while there were days when it felt like I'd Lysoled my fingerprints off and was drowning in behaviors and feelings and conflict. On those days we dramatically altered routines and pursued the light yoke for our family's sake, reprioritizing, reworking homeschool, shelving the unnecessary to buckle down into the deeper, more important stuff, like character, joy, and peace.

So it's a dangerous thing to step into your calling and let the Spirit take over the rooms of your house and your heart. The place gets crowded with growing pains and it wrecks any preconceived notion we ever had about what our lives were supposed to look like. The unexpected often happens, and when it does, sometimes we're too sharp with each other. Frustration and bickering bluster the day away, and criticism chills hearts that should love each other. We just want to give the answer and fix things quickly. Or maybe we want to be seen as someone who has all the answers, overflowing with unwanted advice and unsought council. *That person is doing things differently than I would do them. I would never do it that way...they must need my input.*

> *In nothing is the power of the dark lord more clearly shown than in the estrangement that divides all who still oppose him.*
>
> – J.R.R. Tolkien [1]

One of the slimiest tricks of the enemy is getting us — kids and adults, spouses and friends — to attack each other with discouragement, misunderstanding, ignorant judgment, or anger. He's constantly on the lookout to divide and conquer God's people so we will take each other out. When we fall for it, we all lose.

We're made to win this, though. As an adoptive family working through attachment issues, we were learning to live this daily:

> *We look at our fellow men far too much from the standpoint of our own prejudices. They may be wrong, they may have their faults and foibles, they may call out all the meanest and most hateful in us. But they are not all wrong; they have their virtues, and when they excite our bad passions by their own, they may be as ashamed and sorry as we are irritated. And I think some of the best, most contrite, most useful of men and women, whose prayers prevail with God and bring down blessings into the homes in which they dwell, often possess unlovely traits that furnish them with their best discipline. The very fact that they are ashamed of themselves drives them to God; they feel safe in His presence. And while they lie in the very dust of self-confusion at His feet, they are dear to Him and have power with Him.*

– Elizabeth Prentiss [2]

We must be savvy and kind, not forgetting that we're on the same side. Heaps of grace on each of us, and to each other. The battle is won when we have each other's back.

A new school year loomed and we were more intentional than ever to leverage great books and curriculum and eliminate twaddle that carried any hint of "boys will be boys" or low standard, sin-condoning messages. I needed it for myself, too. We needed joy, kindness, and beauty. Gritty reality needed to be balanced with truth in love. For us, that meant the manipulative bickering of Ramona and Beezus was out, and I was on the lookout for books that showed respectful family relationships and realistic consequences, like those by Edith Nesbit, Louisa May Alcott, and, well, most classics. They were written in an era that expected kids to be both courteous and responsible, instead of winking at minor infractions that grew into major problems.

We were looking for characters in fiction and reality who discerned truth from half-truth, and made the right choice without compromise. We wanted those who, when they made mistakes, refused to justify it by distorting their sense of justice, safety, and obedience. It was our fervent hope that our multi-colored littermates – not the kittens, but the Mexican-Irish-Bulgarian Americans – would gather together with mutual purpose, and grow to be men and women of greatness.

The kittens, though? They ate paper and destroyed lampshades. They climbed curtains and pant legs and bare legs. They attacked the strings of hoodies we wore and pens we wrote with. They hit the caps lock on my keyboard while I typed on autopilot, changing my document midstream. The amount of ridiculous things overheard in our house went up by about two hundred percent:

"Stop chewing on wood chips!"

"Get out of the avocado plant!"

"Mom, Bingley's sucking on the toilet brush!"

Also, apparently we needed to feed the kittens more often.

But whether the assignment was to give a kitten a bath, dose them with dewormer, or remove them from a tight spot they'd gotten stuck in, we followed these directions (or a close variation) every single time:

Collect a few towels. Put a fresh box of bandages nearby. Arm yourself with your widest range of Christian-approved profanity. And get ready to rumble.

Or, an alternative to all that: Wait until your husband is home, and make him do it.

But I went with the first option and learned that God made kittens adorable so you could forgive them when they drew blood with their little bitty meat hooks. All over my right hand, between fingers, around the side of my palm – only two of the gashes were in places that could actually be bandaged. Most of it had to be exposed because covering it would have caused more pain than it was worth.

It resembled our life. There's no one-size-fits-all process with kids, adoption, or special needs. No quick-fix bandaid covers the bleeding, and when we hide all the damage, people assume there's no problem in the first place. Transparency and privacy is a fine line to walk; we prayed that people would remember that most of our wounds weren't visible to the public.

Many adoptive and special needs families are misunderstood, frequently under attack, and struggling with depression. Often churches, family members, organizations, and professionals make well-meaning attempts without really knowing how to help, and sometimes the resources in place to help families actually end up causing more pain because of their ignorance. A lot of these families – more than you might think – eventually quit going to church.

> *Anytime someone asks what the greatest difference in our life is, my #1 answer is church. That is what we gave up in order to answer the call to adopt. It is also what I hear over and over again from [special needs adoptive] families....church is*

> *what they miss the most. It is very sad that the one place or group of people that should be the greatest support and most welcoming place is the one we're often isolated from the most.*

– anonymous adoptive mom

A friend of mine wrote that, and they are hard words to read. So much is at stake.

Some of the damage adoptive families face has to be exposed because covering it causes more harm than healing. So I wrote a series about it, and as those posts went live every day I received emails from adoptive parents and other family members working through attachment. They realized they weren't alone. They realized their situation was common, but just rarely talked about. And they realized there were ways to communicate their family's very special needs to the communities around them that they desperately needed support from. In turn, some of these communities started to understand adoptive families a little better, and they began rallying around them with real help that respected those oh-so-important boundaries that were in place for their child's healing.

That blog series turned into an ebook, and then a self-published book, and then it went through a couple more editions and a bunch of publicity. And even though I sort of always wanted to be an author, I never intended to start by writing about such a private, painful topic.

That October, for the first time in two years, I stood during worship and enjoyed the full benefit of our church's childcare ministry. All the little kids were in their classes, and as we sang "I will fear no evil for my God is with me" my biggest distraction was trying to live that out in the moment and not freak out about the potential fallout from this experiment.

Andrey and Reagan had sat with us in church for two years. We attempted Sunday School classes for them when we first brought them home, quickly realized our error, and had kept them with us ever since. It wasn't the church's fault; we just weren't ready. But we'd spent two years learning and communicating, and then several weeks training and doing more communicating, and lo and behold: Reagan joined her class at church. So far, so good – no fallout, no backlash. It was a huge victory, and one more way God was streamlining things to prepare us for something new.

So we went all crazy radical and let Andrey go to class, too – which led me to the verse of the day, friends:

> *And we know that for those who love God all things work together for good, for those who are called according to his purpose.*
>
> *– Romans 8:28*

How did it go? Let's just say...it wasn't a victory for him. But it was a wonderful, safe opportunity for failure. We learned, the staff and volunteers learned, and our kid learned, and grace abounded for all of us as we navigated the details of care and communication. And we called it good. It worked together for his good, for our good, for our church's good, because God doesn't waste a thing. Not our past, not our mistakes, not our ignorance, and not the sins of others – nothing is wasted. In the stewardship of heaven it is used for good, and turned in our favor.

Even small setbacks and seemingly simple errands – a missed appointment, wasting time in traffic, or just dropping off a movie at the kiosk – are details that are often divinely dealt with, orchestrating time and events like notes in a song that come to play in just the right moment. His timing is perfect; He doesn't sway His plans due to our opinions about the dissonance.

> *I want you to know, brothers, that what has happened to me has really served to advance the gospel, so that it has become known throughout the whole imperial guard and to all the rest that my imprisonment is for Christ.*
>
> *What then? Only that in every way, whether in pretense or in truth, Christ is proclaimed, and in that I rejoice.*
>
> *Yes, and I will rejoice, for I know that through your prayers and the help of the Spirit of Jesus Christ this will turn out for my deliverance.*
>
> *– Philippians 1:12-13, 18-19*

Big leaps in progress with Andrey and Reagan were often met with significant regressions in other areas. For some reason they came hand in hand, like a baby fussing more during a growth spurt. But in order for them to grow and experience victory, we had to risk failure, even though we would all live with the consequences of it. The dissonance was covered with the grace of a brilliant God who can handle both our mistakes, and those of others.

15: curveball

```
October 26, 2014

God has made it clear that I need to
close several pursuits - no more writing
for that magazine, no more selling adorable
knit hats online - and life is greatly
streamlined. This sudden simplifying has me
curious...intrigued. Like He's making room
for something significant, and if He's
doing it, I'm trusting that it is good,
Ephesians 3:20-21 style, more than we can
ask or imagine.
```

We had been waiting for fall with its cold days and hot tea, and then we waited for a quiet afternoon between work and school hours. And now it was finally time: We started reading *Lord of the Rings* to the kids. I would fist-pump the air to show you my enthusiasm, but that would be decidedly non-Elvish.

It wasn't our first go round, but this was the first time all of us read it aloud together. It is a book for fall – for starting in the fall, at least – and then to revel in for the rest of the winter as we trekked through all 1200-something pages on cold nights and snowy afternoons.

You probably know the story: The fate of Middle Earth rests on the destruction of the One Ring, and Frodo has it. He is a wealthy hobbit with a coveted home in the Shire, and he can refuse to take on the task and pass it on to someone else, or ignore all the signs and warnings and pretend life is just fine for as long as possible. But he accepts the mission (you knew that) and he goes all in – giving up his home, his community, and his comfort.

> *"I wish it need not have happened in my time," said Frodo.*
>
> *"So do I," said Gandalf, "and so do all who live to see such times. But that is not for them to decide. All we have to decide is what to do with the time that is given us."*
>
> – J.R.R. Tolkien [1]

And we wish certain things hadn't happened in our time, also. I wish I never had to explain to our kids what abortion is, what human trafficking is, why their brother acted the way he did sometimes, or why their sister has misshapen toes and FAS. There were a million different questions I wish didn't need explaining, and a million different missions I wish didn't need to exist. But they do.

Would it be easier to not adopt? Not to give? Not to go? Not to follow the call He's placed on us? Heck yes, but only in the short term. Long term, it would lead to destruction, and that short-term ease would be dearly paid for by those who are counting on us not to shrug our shoulders.

> *Let each of you look not only to his own interests, but also to the interests of others. Have this mind among yourselves, which is yours in Christ Jesus, who, though he was in the form of God, did not count equality with God a thing to be grasped, but emptied himself, by taking the form of a servant, being born in the likeness of men.*
>
> *– Philippians 2:4-7*

Oh, my friends – you who have followed the Lord's call have pivoted the direction and destiny of the world, for good, forever. You who have slept on hard beds and eaten weird foods in a strange country have changed the future of nations by bringing hope and healing. You who have emptied a vacation account to give to the hungry or heartbroken have planted seed that will grow and proliferate.

Our hands, and many of yours, are in the mud all the way to our elbows. The grit is under our nails and we know we weren't called to easy; we were called to abundance.

Learning to steward abundance is a huge learning curve, though. So in case anyone still thinks we ran a meticulously tight ship, let me share an example of how the boys' bedroom chore went at this season in our lives:

Me: "Did you clean under your bed?"

Son: "Yes…well, I don't remember. I think so."

This is a sure sign that the actual answer is no.

So we go check. A pile of miscellanea in the middle of the floor has already been retrieved, but I crouch down to peek into that dark underworld beneath the bed, and can clearly see that there is more still needing to be rescued.

"What are you going to do with all this?" I ask. Shirts, papers, books, a broken clothes hanger.

"I dunno where any of it goes, so I'm just gonna put it all in a baggie." Aha. Clever. But…

"The shirts?"

"Well, I'll hang those."

I'm picking through, finding broken pens and dowel rods. *Note to self: Hide favorite pens, stop letting boys have dowel rods in their room.*

"All this stuff isn't going to fit in a baggie," I tell him. "You're going to have to put it away in the right places."

"I have extra baggies."

Oh, of course. Perfect solution. *Addendum: Stop giving baggies to Afton.*

It took several attempts, but he finally put everything away in the right places. It was supposed to be a weekly chore, but the job was bigger than he expected and he'd been taking a bi-monthly approach to it. And this, too, is life: Sometimes we know exactly what we're getting into, but most of the time we don't. The cost is higher, the wait is longer, the deadline is shorter, or the assignment is messier.

> *He soon found that the thicket was closer and more tangled than it had appeared. There were no paths in the undergrowth, and they did not get on very fast. When they had struggled to the bottom of the bank, they found a stream running down from the hills behind in a deeply dug bed with steep slippery sides overhung with brambles. Most inconveniently it cut across the line they had chosen. They could not jump over it, nor indeed get across it at all without getting wet, scratched, and muddy. They halted, wondering what to do...*
>
> *"Look!" he said, clutching Frodo by the arm. They all looked, and on the edge high above them they saw against the sky a horse standing. Beside it stooped a black figure.*
>
> *They at once gave up any idea of going back.*
>
> – J.R.R. Tolkien [2]

We don't have to know all the unexpected details. If God had told us ahead of time, we might never have started in the first place. Or maybe we would've quit halfway, just pigeonholing the unpleasant parts of the assignment into a baggie.

But we weren't designed to be quitters or those who shrink back. And this was gnawing at me, because I knew I was shrinking back. I knew I wanted to quit, and I was overwhelmed with shame and guilt for wanting it. I knew that the fear that kept me in bed in the mornings and the hardening in my heart toward the kids and the zoning out in mindless scrolling on social media were all examples of shrinking back. The roiling burnout of compassion fatigue and decision fatigue and physical fatigue – *so much fatigue* – compounded with hypervigilance and trauma had accrued all sorts of darkness within me, and I stopped trusting that God was going to make this better.

I wrote from my couch in the quietness of the wee hours, after the kids were in bed. The writing was a desperate move; I had to hear God's words and I usually heard them best while writing. But the hope, peace, joy, and victory I often wrote about was mostly for an audience who needed it, not for myself. I mean, I needed it, of course. But I did not fully believe it for myself, and I couldn't admit that publicly without compounding the sin of faithlessness with the sin of modeling it for others and making it contagious. So I didn't talk about it to anyone, not even Vince.

One afternoon that November I was on the couch, flattened with fatigue, and Vince was at work. It was just me and six kids. The exhausted prayer came out in two words: *Peace, Lord.*

In these moments, I found myself mentally counting them out again — one-two-three-four-five-six — like I used to back when having six kids was still new, always thinking I was missing someone while trying to keep track of everyone: who was grouped together, who was supervising the Littles, who was in the bathroom and would need either assistance or supervision in the next ten minutes.

And on this evening, the inventory went like this:

Two boys were in their room. I trusted that they were doing what they were supposed to be doing and not doing anything too far outside that criteria, because I was too tired to make the trek up the stairs to check. *Peace, Lord.*

One girl was in the shower and one girl was on the potty, and I was confident that both would be occupied in each of those places for a while. Another girl was with me on the couch, and one boy was eating a piece of candy for dessert. And there was peace...until I heard suspicious giggling from the boys' room.

God was teaching me that peace is something we have to fight for. We mistake it for the quiet calm of rest – and it is that, often, but it is also the hard-fought courage we cling to when we can't do anything else.

The peace we fight for is the peace that has to be learned. It's not the lull quietly handed to us on a silver platter, or a talent we're naturally gifted with. It is the stubborn stillness that refuses to give in to fear and anxiety in the midst of chaos and questions.

> *Rejoice in the Lord always; again I will say, rejoice. Let your reasonableness be known to everyone. The Lord is at hand; do not be anxious about anything, but in everything by prayer and supplication with thanksgiving let your requests be made known to God. And the peace of God, which surpasses all understanding, will guard your hearts and your minds in Christ Jesus.*
>
> *– Philippians 4:4-7*

And I still counted one-two-three-four-five-six, but now I knew what I was missing then: Seven.

God had been speaking to us, and in spite of surgery and health issues that should've made it impossible, He clearly said we were missing someone. He threw a curveball and we caught it, stunned. He *had* been making room for something good, and next summer there would be another addition at our house, even though it seemed like the worst place possible to bring a new baby into.

I raged and wept for all the wrong reasons. I couldn't do this; I already wasn't able to do what I was currently doing. Didn't God see I was failing? Didn't He see how alone we were? What was He thinking to put a baby into this environment of trauma and depression and mayhem?

I knew I should be grateful. I knew this was a gift. I had been a pro-life advocate for years but this was a type of crisis pregnancy I'd never encountered. Choosing to face the turmoil was already daunting, and I had often thought about just not trying anymore. I had been flailing and sinking with every new wave, and could not see land ahead.

I hadn't told anyone. I hadn't even confessed it in my journal, and it was years before I told Vince, before he understood the brink I had been hovering at. But in the dark recesses I had considered some terrible alternatives.

And now, light in the form of a new life had slipped in. It wasn't the first time God sent a baby into darkness to save.

Suddenly my selfish deliberations were no longer an option. The Lord's intense kindness – which seemed anything but kind at the time – led me to repentance.

> *The future, good or ill, was not forgotten, but ceased to have any power over the present. Health and hope grew strong in them, and they were content with each good day as it came, taking pleasure in every meal, and in every word and song.*
>
> – J.R.R. Tolkien [3]

The morning after our positive pregnancy test there was the most beautiful sunrise, and this note was on the bathroom counter waiting for me:

> Well, well, well. What have we here? I'm trying hard to think of what to say. How do I encourage you and make you smile on this most emotionally turbulent morning?
>
> Fear, which should have no place at Copperlight Wood, mixed with expectation of joy, which we have been lacking of late, seem to be at an impasse. What to do? All I can think of is to quote Master Samwise:
>
> "But you haven't put yourself forward; you've been put forward. And as for not being the right and proper person, why, Mr. Frodo wasn't, as you might say, nor Bilbo. They didn't choose themselves."
>
> I can't express how proud, thankful, and impressed I am by you. You're amazing and strong and I love you so very much. Love the Lord, embrace your kids, and let the Holy Spirit lead the way. The enemy fears you. It's not the other way around.
>
> – Vince

The next day was Sunday, and the sermon was on laboring toward the promise, because His promises are guaranteed. We sang *You make me brave* and I wiped my eyes, feeling anything but brave. But in the days since, there had been peace.

Peace, Lord.

Back in January I had written out some notes while praying, not knowing what they were about:

```
What if He puts a door in front of you
that's not on your list?
What if He keeps asking you about it, and
you've considered, thought about it, and
decided against it because of this, that,
and the other?
Maybe there's something He has made
available to you – only you – and it's not
just a doorway opening, but it's more like…
an elevator?
People reject the ride by the thousands
daily.
This, that, and the other are all rooted
in fear. The world would call it caution,
or even wisdom, but the wisdom of men is
foolishness to God.
The world would say, "Sure, maybe it's an
elevator, but it goes both up and down. And
you don't know which direction it's headed
when you step on it."
But...God. God says it's an elevator that
goes down only one level, but up by thou-
sands. And it only goes down for that
moment of transition, preparation — time
enough to put on your shades and hold on
tight before you are raised to where the
sun is brighter.
There's this little something He keeps
asking me to consider. It's foolishness to
men, and only by God does the opportunity
even lay before us. But it's there, and
He's asking. There's no negotiation, no
manipulation — just wonder, and waiting for
confirmation.
```

So God had asked, and we answered, not quite knowing what the question was (yeah, this was becoming a theme) and He must have been enthusiastic because He responded quicker than we expected, before we even thought we were ready. Do we ever think we're ready, though?

We thought we were done, and had donated all of our baby equipage.

He's asking some of you, too — not necessarily the same question He asked us, but something out of the blue, just for you, just because you also were not made to shrink back. You aren't finished. You were made to go forward, to pursue peace and joy deeply, in the way that has to be fought for. You weren't made for the cushioned path, where ease is the counterfeit of peace and diversion is the substitute for joy. You and me...we were ordained to hunker down, cling in close. We were made to connect with the curveball, and go forward.

Few decorations, no baking, no projects, no formal dinner. Christmas was so far from perfect that year. But one part stands out — Christmas Eve, just sitting on the couch next to my grandma, holding hands. Asking her how she was feeling. Her asking me how I was feeling. Talking about cats, hers and ours. Taking turns demurring more food and sweets, and eating seconds anyway. She was 83 that Christmas, and I had just turned 38. On my birthday she pointed out that our ages mirrored each other.

We sat in the living room and listened to her reminisce with my dad and uncle, and they got to talking about collecting pine knots in the woods for firewood when the boys were little. *What are pine knots?* I asked, having often heard of them but never knowing what they were. I've lived in Alaska all my life and we have spruce trees, not pine. But Grandma and Grandpa lived in Arizona before coming up here with four sons.

Pine knots, they told me, are what is left after a pine tree has fallen and rotted away. They are the tough joints and sinew where the branches were attached to the trunk, and when the rest of the tree decomposed, these knots endured the weather and decay. Good fuel, Grandma said – small, but burned forever, and smelled better than the creosote from the old railroad ties they often had to burn.

This brave woman, just under five feet tall now, brought those boys to Alaska and was often on her own as she raised them amid all their shenanigans. And she wasn't finished; she still had one more boy to go. Grandma still sees so much though her vision has been failing. Her eyes are bluer than mine.

I thought back on all of this while sitting with Gus, our striped cat, who used to be shared equally between our oldest son and myself. But between the two of us sitting on the couch, he almost always came to my end and climbed on my lap, heedless of the shrinking real estate due to a pregnant tummy. Maybe it was because of Sophie's absence, or the kittens' presence, but I think it really just boiled down to comfort. He was older, a little bonier, stiffer, and less tolerant of sudden moves and loud noises. He wanted the gentle touch of the mama-friend, not the rough scrubbings of kids who had yet to learn empathy wrought by pain or age.

We are like this, too, in our seasons of rawness. When we are tender and fragile, we naturally lean toward the friend who wields words and truth gently, who holds wisdom humbly because they won it through pain without allowing bitterness to fester. A heart that is ready to be comforted runs to the friend who carries compassion forged through experience.

A few weeks earlier when I called Grandma to tell her about our surprise due midsummer, I wondered what she would say. I wondered if she would discourage me without meaning to when I already felt so brittle.

Why do we do this, bracing ourselves against discouragement even from those we've learned to trust most? But I did brace myself, and told her.

And she asked, "How old are you now?"

Here it is, I thought. "Umm. Almost 38."

"Ohh..." I could hear her smile. "That's a good age...not too old, not too young. I was, oh, 41 when I had Mark. And he was so special, such a gift. A surprise, too, but such a joy. You are –" she paused, I heard a sigh over the phone — "so very blessed."

Exhale.

You are so very blessed.

She saw. She knew I was anxious, and she knew what to say to speak life, comfort, and encouragement. She was referring to my uncle, their fifth boy, the only one born in Alaska. He was born in the same place I was, just five years earlier.

We can know things for ourselves but still need to hear them from others. We can encourage each other with truth and fight each other's darkness, but still need others to shine that truth into us on the days that fall pitch black. We stumble and get our hands and knees in the mud, and a fellow traveler says, *Here, I'll hold your lantern for you while you get back up again. There you are. Bravely now, onward.*

And that Christmas Eve we sat on my dad's couch and held hands. On the other side of her was my uncle, the last one born in the States before they moved here. Our kids played with cars behind the couch and we forgot to bring our camera and it was just a small gathering in this season that felt incomplete from the very beginning. And still, it was perfect.

These curving seasons are what make our story endure. They are the turns, the branchings-off, the connections that make us of the tough sinew that lasts, uncorroded and unwasted. We burn brighter because of them.

For the unsettled family who doesn't know where they'll be going in six months but they know they won't be staying where they are, or for the grieving family who had no preparation for the loss they are suddenly facing, or for the parents making choices they never thought they'd have to consider for their children, or for the single person confronted with unknowns beyond reckoning, or for the mama facing an unexpected pregnancy while still overwhelmed with an alphabet soup of special needs and health issues... may we be the friends who hold wisdom humbly.

This is the season to speak truth in tenderness. This is the time to speak life into darkness for ourselves and for each other. Oh, my friends: This is the day to face things bravely.

> *But I suppose it's often that way. The brave things in the old tales and songs, Mr. Frodo: adventures, as I used to call them. I used to think that they were things the wonderful folk of the stories went out and looked for, because they wanted them, because they were exciting and life was a bit dull, a kind of sport, as you might say. But that's not the way of it with the tales that really mattered, or the ones that stay in the mind. Folk seem to have been just landed in them, usually — their paths were laid that way, as you put it. But I expect they had lots of chances, like us, of turning back, only they didn't. And if they had, we shouldn't know, because they'd have been forgotten.*
>
> – J.R.R. Tolkien [4]

May we be unflinching, not shrinking back, but moving in bold obedience to the curves and bends in our story. *You are so very blessed.*

Most of it is not what we planned, and that is okay. Heroes are not made in control groups living inside a sterilized petri dish. They are made in the wild. They are those who choose to lean hard into the curve instead of turning back.

16: the space between two joys

We passed the darkness of winter solstice, made it to the end of the first trimester, and got through Christmas, which, as you might know, is an achievement for any family. But it felt especially so for one working with attachment challenges and two new kittens and an exhausted mama whose only superpower was the ability to nap on the couch through the uproar of two boys raking through a living room floor that was ankle deep in Legos. I could not, however, sleep through a five-year-old who came within inches of my face to serenade me with "Hark! The Herald Angels Sing."

It was a Christmas of firsts, though: It was the first year our Christmas tree ever toppled over. Remarkably, it was also the first year none of our Christmas ornaments broke, which was probably because it was also the first year we never put out anything breakable. Nativity, candles, ceramic snowmen, glass ornaments, all were still packed away in the crawlspace, protected from kids and kittens.

I emerged from the haze of morning sickness and started to think in full sentences again. The sight of a computer screen no longer caused instant nausea and I longed to write again (but not necessarily in full sentences) and find a little more energy to do things I couldn't even think about before, no matter how desperately they were piling up: the books on shelves leaning every which way, the stacks of papers, notebooks, and reminders piled on a desk that no longer had room for so much as a laptop, and the spilled dirt from a kitten's mess. (Black kitten: nineteen; potted plant on top of bookshelf: zero.)

I even started to think about cooking again. Or at least thinking about food. Or at least thinking, period. It was all progress.

And thinking...well, that's dangerous business. Not all of those thoughts that run in our head, waking or sleeping, are ours. We need a filter that takes them captive, holding them up to the light to see if truth shines through.

Late one night as I was falling asleep, I got caught somewhere in that nebulous realm of free association – that's when you're thinking of, say, the pizza you had for dinner, which reminds you of your favorite pizza place, which reminds you of the wind that nearly knocked you off your feet the last time you went there, which reminds you of flying a kite, and the next thing you know, you're singing "Let's Go Fly a Kite" in your sleep and hearing the soundtrack to *Mary Poppins* in your head all night long.

But that night it was less innocent and I found myself hashing out painful memories from a difficult past relationship. Before I knew it, there were old feelings of pain, shame, regret, and grief, those things long packed away to keep me from breaking, and I just barely caught them in time to recognize the attack that was trying to send me to a place I'm no longer bound to go. Late at night, especially when we're exhausted, weak, or sick, we are vulnerable and must be on our guard.

As I was praying through it and receiving the healing that comes at the speed of thought, I realized that the other person in that relationship (whom I've long since reconciled with) deals with similar attacks, though more numerous and without His truth to ward them off. And I was praying for those who don't know Him at all or don't know Him well, knowing that if *I* wrestle with pain and grief, how much more must those without Jesus wrestle, accepting the harassment as a customary part of life, having only a foundation of thin ice over choppy waters.

We know the truth, but we must also pray and speak it into others. And this applies to our kids so acutely.

I want Andrey and Reagan to be so solid in who they are in Him as they get older and tackle questions about their birth family, origins, and past, that His unchanging truth will be a firm foundation and they will not be shaken by anything else. I prayed they would know that their identity (as loved, adopted, redeemed, and valued) is unchanged by other facts or circumstances. We pray this for all of our kids as they enter adolescence, with its introspection and pursuits to understand their roles in life.

If we can let go of our resentment of others' choices against us and the shame of our choices against others and ourselves, we'll no longer feel bound or limited by the past. We'll refuse to take on bitterness from mistakes, realizing that none of it has limited God or shrunk His influence and plan in our lives. We are learning not to fret over timing and logistics in our decisions about the future, trusting Him in peace to give us wisdom in the perfect time.

> *If any of you lacks wisdom, let him ask God,* **who gives generously to all without reproach,** *and it will be given him. But let him ask in faith, with no doubting, for the one who doubts is like a wave of the sea that is driven and tossed by the wind.*
>
> – James 1:5-6

Without reproach means He doesn't look down on us for asking. He doesn't get annoyed with us for needing it. He gives it abundantly when we are humble enough to admit our need, but He expects us to trust that it *is* given once asked for. And if He's given us the answer, we need to stop asking Him the same question over and over (it drives me nuts when my kids do that, too).

We let natural consequences have their important lessons, like when a child learns not to throw a tantrum on an icy deck where stomping leads to slipping and falling. This is usually how we learn to do the hard thing, all the way through, and do it right. We don't have to do everything; we only have to do what He calls us to today, this minute. Not anything else. You can do this. I can do this.

Reagan, working on fine motor skills, could do this as she kept the pencil on the dotted line all the way around the circle, working hard not to slip. Even my boys could do this as they cleaned out their closet instead of just smushing books and papers behind their clothes. And I could do this as I learned to not focus on what someone else should've done or ought to be doing, but to focus on what I needed to be doing right now, in the moment.

Apparently one of those things I needed to be doing was cleaning out the refrigerator more often. Because we were usually pretty good about using up leftovers and not having science experiments in the fridge, but twice now we had accidentally fermented pineapple.

It was fine, though; we'd been learning a little about probiotics and after some cautious investigation we discovered that it was not only edible, but full of beneficial microorganisms. Usually a bit more planning is involved to turn foods into healthy fermented goodness, but you can also do it by completely avoiding the kitchen during seven weeks of morning sickness.

One afternoon while I researched all that, Cham brought me a book to read to her. She wanted *Fancy Nancy* – and well, it could be worse. (*Amelia Bedelia*, I'm looking at you.) But still, I was in the middle of something.

"Oh...do you really want to read that?" I asked. "Don't you want to learn about water kefir instead?"

"No." As in, *No way, you weird loony.*

I gave in, consoling myself by giving every hoity-toity character a voice like Effie Trinket. *May the odds be evah in your favah.*

That week was a vacation, of sorts. It was more of a staycation meant to be a "workation" to finish some projects. It started well, and was going well, until the middle of the week. And without meaning to, it turned into something else with a phone call.

That brave lady I told you about who taught me about folding fitted sheets, homemade soup, and pine knots had taken an early morning trip to the emergency room, and by the time I got there things weren't looking good. A medevac team was on the way to fly her to Anchorage. My dad met me in the lobby and whisked me to her room.

She was unconscious, tubes and lines everywhere. The nurse filled me in and said her heart had stopped for four minutes that morning, and they did CPR and brought her back – and when I heard that, my heart stopped a little, too. I stayed with her till the medevac team came. She was freezing; I kept my hand on her forehead and prayed. I kept asking the medics if I needed to leave, if I was in their way, and they said *No, you're just fine,* and worked around me, priming lines, switching out bags of fluids and medications, and passing instructions to each other. I whispered in English and prayed in tongues over my Baptist grandma for thirty minutes, until they were ready to put her on the other stretcher and wheel her outside.

I was in the parking lot on the phone with Vince when the helicopter lifted off, and I watched her fly.

We spent several days on alert, on the phone, on our knees. That first day I was fine and faithful, but the second day turned somehow and I was in tears constantly. I plowed through typing up the kids' curriculum for the new term, and realized I was crying. I finished submitting *Upside Down* for paperback, remembered Grandma, and cried again. I did the dishes, wiping my eyes with the same towel and didn't even care. The whole day alternated between tears and productivity. Repeat. Repeat.

> *Blessed is the man who remains steadfast under trial, for when he has stood the test he will receive the crown of life, which God has pro-mised to those who love him.*
>
> *– James 1:12*

*Know Jesus, know peace...*but even still, that peace has to be fought hard for when we confront loss, and not everyone is equipped the same way to handle it. For some it looks like control or anger, in the same way insecurity often looks like pride or narcissism. For others, fighting fear looks like grief on edge.

A mother watches a son fall further into depravity, and she grieves and prays. A woman faces betrayal, fear, and upheaval, and a community prays for a family's future and safety. A city rides out suspense, unnerved over terrorist threats and lost lives. We face sin that ferments into awful, putrid heartbreak in a million directions.

A Baptist uncle speaks of trusting in God's will and sovereignty, and his charismatic niece speaks of trusting in God's goodness and truth. And really, we're talking about the same things.

We sit and wait, wanting answers in the midst of the emergency, and we either ferment into faith or fear. Our choice determines what we will be when life takes an unexpected turn — enduring or decaying, rising or rotten. Something healthy, or something sickening.

Seven days after her heart stopped, Grandma woke up and did a little physical therapy. The next day my husband sat with her after he got off work and made her laugh. She told him how much she missed her cat, he charmed her socks off, and they prayed together.

> *Behold, we consider those blessed who remained steadfast. You have heard of the steadfastness of Job, and you have seen the purpose of the Lord, how the Lord is compassionate and merciful.*
>
> *– James 5:11*

You are so very blessed. The best way to see in the dark is not to keep stumbling on, but to reflect the One who created light with a Word.

We kept praying, so grateful for progress that amazed doctors and glorified God. This woman in her eighties who finally retired the summer before, who raised five boys and then put in more than her fair share with me — she was the lady they tried to keep sedated. But she kept waking up because you can't keep a good woman down, and the odds are always in our favor.

```
January 29, 2015
```

Exhausted, overwhelmed, drained, and inadequate. Nothing unusual, just the accumulation of taking care of six kids while pregnant and trying to pursue some of my own goals, and feeling like I can barely do one or the other successfully, much less both.

I am supposed to be napping – my own rule – but instead I am asking God why He trusts me with all of these and all of this, plus a new baby, when I have failed so much.

He says, *Because I asked and you said yes.*

I said, But I was stupid and didn't know better.

And He said, *I use the foolish to shame the wise.*

Touché.

He's making me know Him more so I can look more like Him. I'm seeing more of what He did and continues to do as the One who was clamored for, who had to make space to get away, and the people still found Him. I came up here to nap, piled pillows between myself and the door so I could cry in peace, and immediately Iree knocked on the door because Reagan was provoking Cham. And I thought, "Is this Your way of telling me to suck it up and get over myself?" I couldn't even cry in peace.

Tonight it is soup and bread for dinner, then showers. If I had more time, I would read, study, journal more, watch those videos on healing the brain, listen to podcasts, finish those videos on attachment, and maybe feel inspired about homeschooling and mothering again. I'd take the time to have neat handwriting instead of this frantic scribble of jumbled thoughts. Instead, I waste time on the internet in one-to-five minute intervals because there isn't enough time to focus on anything that requires a longer attention span, and the interruptions are unavoidable.

And I hate that I think of their needing or wanting me as interruptions.

I don't know what to do. I think the solution is spending more time with each of the kids (for my heart and theirs, and all the dynamics between us) instead of avoiding them or pushing them away, and striving for my own time. And yes, putting up firm boundaries, too, because burnout is a big part of this. Having a clear delineation of time with each kid and time to rest will ease the frantic, grasping pressure on both sides – them clamoring for me, and all of us clawing at each other.

February 2, 2015

Tearful and fried and I have no idea why. I'm up here to escape for twenty minutes while quiet time winds down. I don't know if this is more depression or just the perfect storm of pregnancy hormones and bickering that has me totally on edge. Fear and overwhelm spike with every argument and act of manipulation, disrespect, and disobedience from the kids.

Maybe, possibly, I'm fried because Reagan has pooped in her underwear almost every day for the last month or so, and three times today already, and we haven't even had dinner yet. And Andrey is refusing to ask for things again and chooses to sneak around, helping himself to things without permission instead.

February 3, 2015

I know what it is. I am a pot full of water set on a low simmer, and when I feel capped by so much lying, noise, and negativity, I boil over. The heat is too high, the lid is too tight, and the pressure is too much. Steam, tears, anger, and snappishness come pouring out.

The Lord told me the most amazing thing last night as I was praying and crying in the shower. My hands were together under

```
the water, palm up and filling, and I re-
membered when once before, years ago, He
told me to stay in His sweet spot to be
filled. But I have felt hopeless - like,
what does that really mean? What does it
look like? Last night He told me to look at
my hands, how one was cupped behind the
other hand, holding it up, covering and
protecting it. He said He is covering me.
And He said, "If you only knew how favored
you are. If you only knew how loved and
protected and covered you are," and I
sobbed.
```

Upstairs, I was trying to implement some hard edges into the day so there wouldn't be so many hard edges in my voice and attitude toward the kids. Gus was next to me and Knightley kept chewing the bottom of the curtain which had become unhemmed and ragged, like how I felt. Straggling, worn, unrepaired.

Not beyond repair, just unkempt. Pregnant and fighting fear over more of this pushing and stretching of my limits, longing for relief and waiting for breakthrough, and honestly wondering if it was out there. On my website, out in the open for others, I was faith-filled and hopeful, but for myself? I'd seen too much of myself and how broken I was. I didn't want to be that kind of mother. Our kids deserved better than that, and that was enough of a reason to pursue Him, to pursue hope, to expect the breakthrough.

I saw a picture that day of a comparison between someone who reads little, someone who reads often, and someone who reads profusely: Each person stood on a stack of books that corresponded to their amount of reading, and they faced a landscape of according height. The person who read little was at grass level and saw trees and flowers. The person who read more could see higher – the smog and dark clouds above the trees, and the decay beyond.

But the third person stood on a stack of books that let him see above the clouds, to the sunlight shining over everything. And our life experiences are like that, too.

Ignorance is bliss for the first person. The second person has seen enough to be cynical and jaded. And in these years, I wavered between the second and third person, treading water at cloud level and often sinking in cynicism. I knew there was more though, if I could only stay above long enough to find a foothold and reach it.

I read this in my devotional:

> *Joy is of two kinds. The Joy born of Love and Wonder, and the Joy born of Love and Knowledge, and between the experience of the two Joys lie disciplne, disappointment, almost disillusion.*
>
> *But combat these in My strength, persevere in obeying My Will, accept My Discipline, and the second Joy will follow.* [1]

I was in the space between the two joys, waiting for the second one to come.

17: how we bake bread

In the lobby of the dentist's office during back-to-back cleanings and exams for all six kids, I read *Pilgrim at Tinker Creek* while Aerosmith chanted "Dream On" from the speaker in the ceiling. Four appointments down, two to go.

So far we had scored one cavity and one referral to an oral surgeon. I was fighting a little fear over that last point but counting my blessings that we'd made it over two and a half years without any major medical issues. Most of the families we knew who had adopted from Bulgaria had already achieved at least one major surgery. We weren't sure what we were dealing with aside from facial swelling, a biopsy, adult teeth overlapping somewhere near Andrey's sinuses, and words like *possible cyst* and *extraction*...but we were certain it had something to do with those first years of starving and neglect, when there weren't enough nutrients to build bone structure to properly fit future adult teeth.

In the speaker overhead, Queen sang about this crazy little thing called love. The irony wasn't lost on me, though I grew up on Dwight Yoakum and prefer his version.

We needed to call the surgeon's office when we got home. Make an appointment for a consultation. Briefly explain attachment issues to a whole new team of professionals in attempt to avoid regression. Brace ourselves for whatever came next.

But for now, I read about the anxiety of unknowing: *When will this end? When will it get better? What happens next?* And there was irony here, too:

risk the ocean

> *I wonder how long it would take you to notice the regular recurrence of the seasons if you were the first man on earth. What would it be like to live in open-ended time broken only by days and nights? ....how long would you have to live on earth before you could feel with any assurance that any one particular long period of cold would, in fact, end?*
>
> *"While the earth remaineth, seedtime and harvest, and cold and heat, and summer and winter, and day and night shall not cease": God makes this guarantee very early in Genesis to a people whose fears on this point had perhaps not been completely allayed.*
>
> – Annie Dillard [1]

Vin brought coffee and baked goods to get me through the last two cleanings. I read more about trees, water, fear, and assurance as I ate a croissant in the lobby and tried not to make a mess. It was the worst possible thing to attempt this with; pastry bark had flaked all over. It would've been more efficient to just rip the thing wide open and fling crumbs everywhere, since that's what it looked like I did anyway.

But two pastries and a latte later – because my cleaning wasn't for another few weeks – we were done, and home, and off the phone. Appointment with the surgeon scheduled for next week.

And we waited, wondered, and prayed. It's what we do when we don't know. *Maybe it won't be so bad. Maybe it's nothing after all. Maybe it will be awesome. Maybe God is up to something.* And of course He's always up to something, but sometimes I cringe because He can be such a troublemaker.

We fought off the what ifs for the meeting, the doctor, the prognosis, the plan. We prayed against fallout and fear, the emotions ripped right open and scattering a mess everywhere.

A week later we learned a little more about what were facing: an adult tooth growing way the heck up under Andrey's eye, and another that seemed encased in a cyst. Putting the medical stuff aside, it was really the trust issues I was most concerned with. *Can we trust this team to handle our son and our family? Can we trust Andrey to handle this? Will he learn to trust us more through this?*

Can we trust God to know what He's doing here?

And the answer is yes. Yes, and yes, and yes, and amen.

At home, Andrey sighed and grunted and stomped over his chore as though he carried the weight of the whole world on his small shoulders in his responsibility to sweep the living room.

You are not carrying the weight of the world, I wanted to tell him.

*I **must** carry the weight of the world,* his behavior said. This is the default attitude of someone who has learned the world is not to be trusted.

You're not in charge of all of this. Often, I did tell him this.

*But I **must** be in charge of everything. If I mind everyone else's business, I won't have to deal with my own.*

We adults have these same conversations with God all the time. Our healing and maturity are indicated by having them less and less often.

We scheduled a CT scan for the following week. The surgeon had talked about a procedure with a four or five day recovery, and then maybe a surgery to extract up to three adult teeth if they couldn't be saved. Long term, he mentioned words like *non-cosmetic orthodontics, extensive restructuring, root canal.*

But short term we prayed, learning to practice a stubborn trust because God is always up to something.

It was almost spring, and chubby chickadees flitted in slim willow trees. While Iree and I threw a quick lunch together, Vincent read *The Little Red Hen* aloud to everyone else. You know, *Who will help me thresh this wheat? Who will help me bake this bread? Not me, says the cat. Not me, says the dog*, and so on.

Lunch was never fancy and this was just bread with cream cheese and veggies, plus a handful of nuts for each plate. The sun was shining and it gave the thermostat delusions of grandeur, boasting 72 degrees in direct light in late March. Iree asked if they could eat out on the deck.

"Sure. All of you guys want to eat outside?" I ask.

Vincent answered, "Not me."

"Says the pig," squeaked Cham. Clever girl.

Pussy willows were growing out there. In here, my belly was growing and old stretch marks came alive again as our littlest resident flexed his muscles. A couple of months earlier when the air was drier, my biggest pregnancy complaint was that I was itchy everywhere from the stretching, and the midwife just told me to drink more water. Sigh.

I thought, Really, that's all you've got? Tell me something more intriguing than that. Tell me something expensive, even. Surely there's a homeopathic something-or-other for dry, pregnant, Alaskan skin that's far more interesting than just "Drink more water."

My raised eyebrows must've communicated all of that for me, because she said, "Yep. More water. Drink more than you think you need, even."

It sounded oddly like something I'd read that week:

> *And Elisha sent a messenger to him, saying, "Go and wash in the Jordan seven times, and your flesh shall be restored, and you shall be clean."*

> *But Naaman was angry and went away, saying, "Behold, I thought that he would surely come out to me and stand and call upon the name of the Lord his God, and wave his hand over the place and cure the leper."*
>
> *– 2 Kings 5:10-11*

Nothing fancy, nothing extravagant – go right over there, to the muddy Jordan. Just wash seven times. More than you think you need to.

> *But his servants came near and said to him, "My father, it is a great word the prophet has spoken to you; will you not do it? Has he actually said to you, 'Wash, and be clean'?" So he went down and dipped himself seven times in the Jordan, according to the word of the man of God, and his flesh was restored like the flesh of a little child, and he was clean.*
>
> *– 2 Kings 5:13-14*

No frills, just obedience. And yet we worry that we're wasting time and spinning our wheels in the monotony of transition: waiting for healing, waiting for birth, waiting for a move, waiting for that next big thing that we've been called to. We make moves and feel like we're going nowhere – or worse, we think we're going backward from making the wrong move, in the wrong time, when we thought we were following directions.

Which sounds like another story I was familiar with:

> *Now the donkeys of Kish, Saul's father, were lost. So Kish said to Saul his son, "Take one of the*

> *young men with you, and arise, go and look for the donkeys." And he passed through the hill country of Ephraim and passed through the land of Shalishah, **but they did not find them**. And they passed through the land of Shaalim, **but they were not there**. Then they passed through the land of Benjamin, **but did not find them**.*
>
> *- 1 Samuel 9:3-4*

What is this all about? *I thought You told me to do X and Y, and then Z would happen. Instead it feels like I'm doing the Hokey Pokey.* Plant the seed. Grind the flour. Dip seven times. Put your right foot in, take your right foot out, put your right foot in, and shake it all about. It all seems so unnecessary.

You said you'd help Me, Jesus tells us. *Hey Love,* **this is how we bake bread.**

> *Now the day before Saul came, the Lord had revealed to Samuel: "Tomorrow about this time I will send to you a man from the land of Benjamin, and you shall anoint him to be prince over my people Israel. He shall save my people from the hand of the Philistines. For I have seen my people, because their cry has come to me." When Samuel saw Saul, the Lord told him, "Here is the man of whom I spoke to you! He it is who shall restrain my people."*
>
> *– 1 Samuel 9:15-17*

Saul thinks he's been wandering and searching to no purpose, but the Lord has been preparing him to reign.

> *Then Saul approached Samuel in the gate and said, "Tell me where is the house of the seer?"*
>
> *Samuel answered Saul, "I am the seer. Go up before me to the high place, for today you shall eat with me, and in the morning I will let you go and will tell you all that is on your mind. As for your donkeys that were lost three days ago, do not set your mind on them, for they have been found.*
>
> *– 1 Samuel 9:18-20a*

All these movements – planting, harvesting, threshing, milling the wheat into flour, and baking just to get bread. Just to be clean. Just to raise kids. Just to get to the place He's been sending us all along.

Our hearts are put out there again and again, only to be crushed, disappointed, bewildered, confused, and the enemy scatters tares of half-truths in attempt to make us misinterpret events. We feel like we've made a misstep or a false start.

The truth, though? God is strategically putting things in order. He's tilling the ground of our heart before we get to what He's been preparing us for all along. Under the surface, deep in the soil, He is softening us, breaking up our clods, making us like Him. Instead of someone fearful of putting our heart out there, He makes us bold, willing, and vulnerable – like Himself, who put His heart out for us over and over.

We're doing more than we think we need to because we're being prepared for more than we thought to ask for.

Our calling is more than we thought it was. We're loved more than we think we know. We have more than we think we need.

I drove home from that routine appointment with our midwife with no worries, no big concerns, no major problems. Some back pain, some heartburn, normal pregnancy woes. The sky over me was blue, but a wall of black clouds loomed toward our house. Cresting the top of the hill on the highway, I saw hail filtered through sunlight falling on the intersection below, and as I stopped at the bottom of the hill a minute later, the sun was still shining but tiny balls of snow were falling everywhere.

The light turned green and cars started to move again. Many of the vehicles coming toward me were covered in fresh snow, a clear warning of the weather ahead. There was sunlight and then darkness, sudden and startling. Hail, rain, and snow, right next to miles of sunlight, temperamental Alaska in all her glory. I drove through town, trying to keep the windshield wipers caught up with the speed of the downpour.

It was like hormones, like adoption, like life; sometimes we have warning, and other times we have no clue what we're driving into, no matter how fast your wipers are flapping. Stress took its toll: Over two and a half years of cortisol flooding my system, and not enough rest or water. I had been sick so often.

Four days later I had emergency surgery at twenty-seven weeks pregnant.

I had just entered the third trimester, and sometimes it still shocked me to realize this was really happening: Our seventh. I mean, we'd had two ultrasounds, my belly kept getting bigger, and I felt him kicking all over the place. But it still didn't really hit me until a friend gave me a pair of teeny-tiny overalls.

Knowing this about myself ought to give me more sympathy for my kids when they have a hard time accepting reality, but it doesn't. Almost every day I found myself repeating an instruction to one of them only to have them say, "You never told me that."

"Yes, I did tell you that," I'd say.

"Well, I didn't *hear* you tell me." And I replied that what I said wasn't dependent on whether or not they were listening. Reality isn't compromised by our level of attention.

And this is a good thing because sometimes our attention is beyond our control. Sometimes it's directed with such force and concentration that everything else diminishes to grey in the background, and nothing else matters.

A few days after I saw the midwife, I came home from an afternoon of other appointments and an odd, bloating pain like I've never felt before started creeping into my midsection. In an hour it had taken over my whole torso. I took a bath, a supplement, and another bath, but it got worse. I even took pain medication, which I never do. I started throwing up around 9:00 pm and didn't stop until after we got to the emergency room around 4:00 am. Nothing mattered but agony beyond anything I'd experienced in natural childbirth, and the fear that crept in with it. The only other time I'd ever been sick from physical pain was when we lost a baby.

Peace that usually covers us like a blanket stretched itself thin and sheer over a situation I had no grasp of.

> *I had said in my alarm, "I am cut off from your sight." But you heard the voice of my pleas for mercy when I cried to you for help.*
>
> *– Psalm 31:22*

After an hour in the ER, peace thickened with the help of intravenous pain meds and the world stopped reeling so fast. Another medication, another doctor. Several nurses. Between the ER, admitting, and Labor and Delivery, I had the same conversation with almost all of them while they filled out paperwork:

"Which pregnancy is this for you?"

"Sixth." *Yes, we are those kind of people. No, we're not Mormon or Catholic. Yes, we know how this happens...and we like it.*

"You have five children already?" they'd ask, eyebrows raised. And this is where the math gets fuzzy even without narcotics.

"No, we have six kids at home," I told them. "Four biological, two adopted. We lost our second baby in a miscarriage...this is our sixth biological baby." I understood their confusion. Like I said, some days I have a hard time grasping all of this, too.

They wheeled me to ultrasound and the tech discovered a gall bladder full of stones. "Enough to make a necklace out of," she said. Oh, goody.

It meant emergency surgery, and the flat-voiced surgeon drew us a picture of what it looked like and what had to be done – incisions, medications, recovery, risks.

"What about our baby?" I asked. "There are two of us here." The Doppler played Finnegan's heartbeat in the background.

"The best way to keep the baby healthy is to keep you healthy. Your gall bladder is extremely sick, it has to come out." And then, the awful warning: "We cannot guarantee he will make it through the surgery."

> *The angel of the Lord encamps around those who fear him, and delivers them.*
> *When the righteous cry for help, the Lord hears and delivers them out of all their troubles.*
> *The Lord is near to the brokenhearted and saves the crushed in spirit.*
> *Many are the afflictions of the righteous, but the Lord delivers him out of them all.*
>
> *– Psalm 34:7, 17-19*

In that terrifying helplessness, the Spirit's voice came: *Hey, Love...I'm right here. I'm going to show up in spite of this. I'm not going anywhere. I don't require your constant focus to be at work when you are under attack.*

Then the surgeon's voice again, saying something about another doctor from Labor and Delivery who would assist the entire time. They would monitor the baby until the surgery began and then again, as soon as it was over. They couldn't monitor him during the procedure, though.

Hey Love...when you're distracted or in pain or asleep, I'm there as much as ever, whether you feel it or not. The pain doesn't keep Me from you. The medication doesn't keep Me from you. My peace is still with you, even when it feels thin enough to be transparent. The peace and protection is My work; your work is to just trust Me.

I woke up after the surgery in a different room, to the sound of Finnegan's heartbeat steadily thumping away on the Doppler monitor. A new nurse sat next to my bed doing paperwork.

"He's okay?" I asked.

She smiled. "Yes, he's just fine."

> *For God alone, O my soul, wait in silence, for my hope is from him. He only is my rock and my salvation, my fortress; I shall not be shaken. On God rests my salvation and my glory; my mighty rock, my refuge is God. Trust in him at all times, O people; pour out your heart before him; God is a refuge for us.*
>
> – *Psalm 62:5-8*

There were no stones to see or admire. The surgeon said the gall bladder was almost gangrenous, falling apart, and they chucked the entire thing after draining it. He also said, "You'll need to take it easy for two weeks. You've got several injuries to heal from." He paused. "Of course, we caused them on purpose, but for good reason."

A bandage covered my belly and my insides felt oddly unsettled because I was missing a small organ. Not that I was ever particularly fond of my gall bladder; I just never thought anything of it.

My work isn't dependent on your memory, your awareness, or your understanding of all the facts.

Sometimes God forces us into the unknown for healing. Had I kept food down, or been able to sleep that night, or the pain subsided at all, we would've stayed home. We might've missed how dire the situation was until maybe too late. Physically and emotionally, He knew there were wounds that needed to be treated with hard boundaries, cut and cauterized, and poisonous connections clipped off. We have no doubt He heals us constantly of things miraculously with and without our awareness, but for some reason, that time He chose to heal through surgery.

We come under attack in various ways and often feel like we can't hear Him when we most need to. But if we are abiding, in the habit of listening and pursuing Him, our momentary hearing doesn't matter because He's already given us the instruction we need.

And I was fine. And our baby, praise God, was fine. But the recovery was wild, and I'm not talking about the incisions or the fact that I was still a little loopy as the drugs wore off. I'm talking about two of our kiddos who had a hard time handling any uproar that wasn't caused by their own behavior. The coming weeks were filled with light and dark, chiaroscuro, sunshine and hail.

18: where breakthrough comes from

Between the husband, kids, and a posse of friends, we had meals made, laundry done, groceries delivered, kids bathed, dishes washed, and the kitchen cleaned. My first night home after the surgery, we tucked the kiddos into bed and the following amazing conversation took place, over two and a half years in the making.

"You already hugged me!" Andrey said.

"I know. I'm hugging you again."

"Because you love me?" he grinned.

Outwardly I was cool, but inwardly I was trying not to faint. "Yes."

But the next day he gave us the virtual middle finger, right and left, at every opportunity. That love thing is terrifying, you know – let's not have too much of that. Both kids had a rough week with one thing after another.

"Mom," Iree said, coming downstairs. "Reagan's up there saying, 'Mommy hit me' and 'Mommy flick me.' And she's hitting and flicking herself, and her laundry is still all over the floor."

And, oh, it made me angry. The part of me that was raised with, *Stop your crying or I'll give you something to cry about* wanted to lash out at her, but it would play right into the enemy's hands because it's what she remembered, still, years later. *Love is scary, so let's create anger because anger is safe and familiar. Push Mommy away before she can leave me.*

That night she refused dinner and threw up all over her bed, and not because she was physically ill. But we'd had months of progress since the last time she did that, so we knew more sunlight was ahead.

> *"I'm just going to love him."*
>
> *"That's the hard way," she said.*
>
> *"With God's help, I want to be something like grace to him. I don't know how the shrink stuff works and I don't want to pretend to know or try a bunch of fashionable strategies. So, if it works, it works, and if it doesn't, maybe he and I will both learn something in spite of ourselves."*
>
> *"You know he's frightened of attachment, of any real closeness. It's what he wants most from you, but he'll keep trying to push you away."*
>
> *"I'm not going away."*
>
> – Jan Karon [1]

Andrey went in for his scheduled surgery first thing in the morning – alas, the hospital did not have a punch card for multiple procedures – and I got my stitches out in the afternoon. We had no other plans involving the hospital anytime in the future, though considering the roundabout behind it and the steep ditch next to its entrance, I'm pretty sure the design was meant to drum up business.

```
April 26, 2015

The Lord just reminded me that in what-
ever we're doing - reading, washing dishes,
or anything mundane or messy that seems to
be a waste of time in life's urgency - our
```

obedience opens us up to hear Him better, and it protects and covers us from attack that we would otherwise be vulnerable to.

I was reading the Bible. And as one part of my brain was reading First Chronicles, another part of it was receiving ideas for writing. Not as a distraction, but as an opportunity to hear the message He has for me in this moment. Our brains aren't limited to the obvious in front of us or only one plane of thought, but He gives us a multidimensional ability to receive from Him, downloading His words for our needs that go beyond the immediate, physical, or academic attempts we're focused on.

For the same reason we associate smells with certain feelings or events, and for the same reason studies show that if students chew the same gum during studying as they do when taking a test, their scores are higher for doing so – our minds are taking in much more all the time than they seem to be doing on the surface.

This interworking is why we can pray for physical and spiritual healing simultaneously over the same situation, even when it seems that the physical and spiritual problems have nothing to do with each other.

Andrey's face, post-surgery, was so grotesquely swollen yesterday after having three teeth extracted and a cyst removed. Physically, we're praying for his healing and comfort, of course. But spiritually, we're also praying for healing over his past and how it affects his present and future, that all of the swollen traumas, insecurities, and wounds would be brought down to size and heal perfectly. We are praying that the inflamed stubbornness and need for control would diminish and stop taking up more space in his life than they ought to. We're praying that spiritual malformation caused by neglect and abuse will be cleaned out just as the cyst was. We're praying for spiritual orthodontics, placing and rearranging all of his mental, emotional, and behavioral needs in an appropriate way in his life.

All of that, from reading two chapters in the Old Testament.

A little black cat joined me upstairs for a bit of reprieve. It had taken ten months but Knightley finally seemed to understand her role as afternoon comforter and bedtime snuggler, although she had no interest in sharing ice cream and infinitely preferred eating our houseplants.

I told the kids I would lay down for a while. I had crazy low iron post-surgery, and the midwife put me on a new supplement to replace one I had just started a month earlier.

"What should I do with the old one?" I'd asked her.

She grinned. "Save it for your next pregnancy."

In a miraculous demonstration of self-control for a woman eight months pregnant with her seventh child, I did not throw the bottle of methylfolate at her head.

So I was resting, but instead of laying down I first finished a bar of chocolate. One serving was a third of the bar, and it had six percent of the daily recommended allowance for iron...so I tripled that with all three servings. All for the sake of nutrition, of course. But baked treats had been disappearing pretty fast, too.

"Mom, did you eat *two* chocolate muffins already? They *just* came out of the oven!"

"Yes..." I confessed, "but Finnegan ate the first one."

Vincent smirked. "Ha, Mom gets extra." (Dear future

daughter-in-law, you are so welcome.)

My bandages from the surgery were gone, replaced by four scars. And the more pregnant I became, the more pregnant we felt for breakthrough, also. Our older cat needed an expensive procedure, the Stagecoach needed a repair, and Vince had jury duty coming up. Special needs and trauma left our home bursting at the seams, desperate for more space so we could divide and conquer behaviors that kept sucking us under.

We had cleaned and nested and purged for simplicity, but the house still felt like your favorite old sweater whose sleeves had shrunk in the wash and no longer fit, despite how comfy it was. Relief had to be coming soon, in some area, somehow.

God had moved mountains to bring this new person here. Moving mountains isn't hard for Him, though it always seems like such a big deal to us. But the movement in our hearts is the real mountain to be overcome. We base our readiness for our callings on feelings and circumstances, and He says those have very little to do with it. We're not ready for something because we feel like it, but because He has plans and has already prepared us for them.

In prayer and prophetic words, the overriding theme was that Finnegan was bringing healing, peace, and restoration to our family. His middle name was Dunamis, meaning, "power, strength, divine ability; the power to restore, heal, and accomplish."

When God plants something in us, it stays in harbor for a while, almost dormant, while we wait for His perfect timing and fruition. I could feel Finnegan rolling in my belly, just as I knew God was stirring other things we labored for into activity and birth. The fullness, swelling, and pain were all signs of imminent delivery, life, and joy – the beginning of what we longed for.

Life is a cycle of labor and delivery: learning to work, and to wait, and to let Him take over when we are at the end of what we can do...and He does.

July 2, 2015

I've been reading about roots and fruits, and how taller plants need deeper roots. And this applies to many things: a pianist practices hours of scales - developing roots - before the concert, which bears the fruit. We grow roots in closet intercession before the fruit of victorious public prayer. Hard parenting moments and tedious discipline grow deep roots before children display the fruit of good behavior in public. Or, the writer plows through every day in private writings before the published works take off. All of the quiet growth happens underground, unseen, but the deeper it goes, the larger the fruit is later.

And in thinking of fruit, my laptop is nearly busted, we have another bill to pay for my surgery (apparently surgeons make $2400 an hour and we are in the wrong business), and our savings is shrinking rapidly. Not sure how to meet all this, and trusting God to provide.

That sounds so calm and confident, but I had a good cry over it a while ago. Maybe it was the requisite pre-labor crying jag. But I finally realized what I was so heartbroken over is that this is not what I wanted - the broken computer right around the birth of our son, the evenings it has taken from us as Vin tried to repair it to no avail, the disobedience from the kids today. None of it should be happening, added to impending labor. Then I really went

off on God, telling Him that while I am of
course grateful for Finnegan, this pregnancy wasn't my plan, and how things with
Andrey and Reagan for the last three years
weren't what we wanted, either.

And He is so gentle. The Holy Spirit
said, *I know. I know what it is to not get
what you want. I know what it is to wrestle
with the Father's will. But I also know
what it is to surrender to it and trust His
will is best – and His will is the best
for you, too. Broken laptops, extra chores,
attachment woes, all of it.*

A couple weeks later I was in bed timing contractions. Vince's head blocked my view of the clock, so I gave him a firm nudge. 8:42 a.m.

He gave me a look. "We've moved a few steps closer to Labor Shannon."

"What? I needed to see what time it was."

"I know, you're losing your filters." *Filters* being a nice way of saying boundaries, manners, and any concern for the personal space or feelings of others. You know, like a pregnant woman in labor.

But later that morning he was on the couch reading to a pile of kids. Cham pointed to a dog in the picture and asked what kind it is.

"A papillon," he said. "They're stupid little dogs."

Over the kids heads, I gave him a look.

"What? It's true," he laughed.

"We've moved a few steps toward Labor Vince. You're losing your filters, too."

It was sort of an encouragement. Maybe we really were close, finally. Finnegan was in a weird position. I'd been in early labor for three weeks with contractions that didn't seem to go anywhere and ligament pain that dropped me to the floor at times. While browsing the internet late one night, I saw an article on "Five Ways to Know if Your Cow is Getting Ready to Calve" and barely repressed a desperate curiosity to see if it had any wisdom for me.

None of that was what I was really anxious about, though.

By the end of the pregnancy, I was not only physically wiped out but I was emotionally uncertain and struggling. *Can I do this? God, what are You thinking?*

I knew all the Bible verses. I knew *with God all things are possible.* But I felt like I was already failing too often.

We fight fear and discouragement when we're not the person we want to be. We have high expectations of ourselves as moms, wives, leaders, artists, ministers, professionals, whatever. And high expectations are good; I'm all for them. But what if our expectations of what we want to be are a skewed version of what God wants us to be? What if our highest expectations are beneath His vision for us?

Is His will good enough for us? Or do we want what we want, when that is all too often what the world dictates for us?

Maybe our family wasn't wrong. Maybe families are *supposed* to take on huge challenges and come to the end of themselves and learn to trust God for radical healing and restoration. Maybe *that's* what's supposed to be normal, rather than the comfortable, spacious lifestyle that lets us be the center of our own universe.

Will we turn down a life fit for glossy magazine pages in favor of a life of transparency? What if we traded our shiny packaging for rough brown paper, tied with grace?

I had just finished reading about King Saul when he was threatened by the Philistines. He was anxious and fearful to the point of outright disobedience to God, taking matters into his own hands and offering a sacrifice he was not authorized to make. And I'm familiar enough with fearful impatience to relate to him.

What really struck me, though, was that the author of the book I was reading [2] said she believed God had all the Philistines show up so Saul could take them all out. The threat was not the end it seemed to be; it was his opportunity for greatness. And he failed that opportunity.

But we don't have to.

Finnegan was born early in the morning, in the water, at the birth center, in the same room his sister had been born six years earlier. After I pushed him out and the midwives handed him to me, I held him, astounded. I had been in such disbelief the entire pregnancy, but there really *was* a baby in there. *The Lord really did this, and brought us through, and here he is.*

And then, a new fear I hadn't even named but had been lurking in the background nonetheless rose to the surface: Would I bond and attach with him? Would he feel unwanted because I had been in such turmoil and disbelief? Did he somehow know that I had cried for all the wrong reasons when the pregnancy test was positive?

Those fears vanished with the first skin-to-skin snuggle. The fuzzy hair, the newborn-soft cheeks, the warmth of his body that had been growing inside my own for months...I breathed it all in and realized how much, how fiercely I wanted him.

And God very tenderly said, *Hey, Love...I told you so.*

> *Then Jacob awoke from his sleep and said, "Surely the Lord is in this place, and I did not know it."*
>
> *– Genesis 28:16*

The midwife adjusted the sheets around us, and said his name, smiling.

"Finnegan. I think he means 'fun again' for your family."

And he did. He smiled and laughed, he bonded and responded. He grew and learned in all the ways babies and little kids are supposed to when they have a healthy start. Finnegan reminded me of how fun motherhood could be, and that I really was a good mom – and that I loved being a mom.

> *I think of the green insect shaking the web from its wings, and of the whale-scarred crab-eater seals. They demand a certain respect. The only way I can reasonably talk about all this is to address you directly and frankly as a fellow survivor.*
>
> *...although we hear the buzz in our ears and the crashing of jaws at our heels, we can look around as those who are nibbled but unbroken, from the shimmering vantage of the living.*
>
> – Annie Dillard [3]

I had been so undeserving, had never recognized the measure of God's forgiveness and mercy in His gift of this boy I love so much. Had He asked us if we wanted to be pregnant again, we would've said, "No thanks. Not now, maybe later." We did, in fact, say "No, thanks" in several ways, and God vetoed us every time. He could have said *Okay, no problem, I'll find someone else.*

We would have missed out, and never known the magnitude of the gift we'd turned down.

But God didn't ask us, and we had this little life to show for it. As I type this eight years later, I'm still undone by gratitude. This life isn't what we wanted, and I am immeasurably glad He gently forced us to surrender to it anyway. We did not know then that breakthrough comes through more of the battle, not less of it.

19: the long view

She woke up with one question.

"You say, 'Happy bootday, Reagan?'"

After 364 days of talking about what she wanted to do on her birthday – to the point we had to reign in and discipline it lest she drive herself and the rest of us crazy – we finally we got to say, *Yes. Happy bootday, Reagan. Today is your day.*

"Do you know how old you are?"

She grinned and fluttered her hands. "Yes!"

"How old are you?"

"Five!! I *five*, mama!"

Yep. Still working on that.

She was born ten years earlier, when Andrey's biological mom was seven months pregnant with him, and I was six months pregnant with Afton. During their first five years, we didn't know Andrey or Reagan existed. And during the next five years, we spent two trying to bring them home, and the next three helping them know they *were* home. For good, forever.

She opened her first gift and before I knew it I heard myself say, "Do you like it?" Suddenly it was three years earlier when I was asking the same thing in my best awkward Bulgarian. *"Haresva li ti?" Please say yes. Please mean it.*

And she did like them. Vin took a risk and bought size eight pants; they were way too long and would fit nicely in the top of her closet while we waited for her to grow into them. But what she really loved came next.

"Oh! *Ohhh*! Hoo-ey, *ahhhsome*! Yay, hoo-ey!" I have never seen anyone so excited over hooey before. (She still loves hoodies. She also loves rocking chairs, cars, and drawing stick figures. What really makes her light up, though, is music...and food, of course.)

Vin was home for the day; eight inches of fresh snow covered everything and it was still coming down on our cusp of the valley. We had a snowball fight before lunch – all of us except Reagan, who wasn't interested. She made tracks, ate snow, and watched from a safe distance. Cham also wasn't interested, so she made herself a snow throne and sat like a queen in the middle of the action, occasionally granting boons of huge snowballs to us, and just as often getting hit in the crossfire with her own artillery.

But Andrey joined us, and for you to understand how significant it was for him do so, I have to tell you that he cried fat tears the first time Vince ever gave him a high five because he thought he was getting hit. The boundaries were so paper thin and fragile sometimes, with us learning to trust him and him learning to trust us.

Vince and I were captains and we chose sides – I took Vincent and Andrey, he took Iree and Afton. Afton captured Andrey and took him to the snowbank, and Vincent and I had to stage a rescue.

Under heavy fire from Vin and Iree, Vincent pushed Afton into the snow bank on their side and I threw (okay, *gently shoved)* Andrey toward the safety of the snowbank on our side. And he loved it. The snow was everywhere – in our eyes, stuck in our hair and melting down our faces, sailing in arcs to land on hats and backs and behinds.

(There was some hand-to-hand combat and it got a little messy. If you ask Vin, he might tell you some nonsense about me playing dirty and shoving a ton of snow down the front of his shirt. But that's ridiculous; I would never have done that because he had Finnegan in the front pack under his jacket. I shoved the snow down the *back* of his shirt…just so we're clear.)

There was soup and bread inside for lunch, then a movie and a nap. A normal, relatively easy day. The next day was harder; behavioral fallout from excitement and change were still super common. Sometimes it was over a routine appointment, and sometimes it took us back to behaviors we hadn't seen since those first weeks together in a hotel in Bulgaria.

Every day was a study: Will they cooperate with school or speech today? Will they have fun? Will they try to isolate from all of us? Will they obey routines, or will they sabotage opportunities for freedom and joy? Will they know that we will do what we can to rescue them from attack, but that we won't rescue them from the consequences of their own actions?

The pendulum still swings, but as the years have passed the fluctuation from one extreme to the other is less violent, tapering more and more as time goes by. As they get older, I hope we'll see the right answers to all these questions. I hope all of our kids will forgive us for being imperfect parents. I hope they will forgive and love themselves. And I hope when it comes time to choose sides, they will choose life.

I hope they will see Jesus through their entire story, protecting, loving, correcting, and renewing. I want them to know He is for them, and wake up every morning to hear Him say, *Hey, Love. Today is your day.*

After that snowstorm, some moose came through our backyard and the mama just stared at us through the window, her ear flickering at sudden noises, on guard nonstop. Her baby was nearby eating a willow. We stared at her, staring at us, as she sized us up.

I know how she felt, this mama on high alert: A little on edge. We constantly watch for danger, trying to keep our kids safe and in sight, trying to rest so we're ready for the next alarming movement that will demand our attention and force us to make sudden, on-the-spot decisions.

Around that time, someone asked me what our family really needs and how the church can support us. It's a loaded question so I gave the easy, predictable answer: *Pray for us.* Then the Spirit pricked me towards transparency, and I also mentioned we needed a bigger house. And it was true, we needed both of those things. But I wish I would've said childcare. Or a meal once a week. Or just, hey, invite me to things even if you think I probably can't come. You'll probably be right, but it's nicer to be invited than to be written off and see all the photos on social media later.

The church is starting to recognize that special needs adoption is a frontline ministry unlike most others. The mission field is brought into the home, and it often (especially in the first years) becomes a war zone. There's no clocking out, no furlough, no sabbatical. There's no leaving triage after a twelve hour shift, and there is no sanctuary or refuge because our homes and lifestyles became utterly devoted to this cause.

I still hear from grieving moms who are walking wounded, marriages struggling, everyone suffering some level of trauma from the chaos. And for the most part, I don't mean families who just recently adopted. I mean families – moms, dads, and siblings – who have been in this for years and have little left after so many miles of driving on rims.

What can we do? A meal once a week, rotated among friends, could free up an hour for the adoptive parents to spend much-needed time doing any number of other things that need caught up on: errands, paperwork, phone calls, one-on-one time with a child, or (gasp!) even alone time to decompress. For reals.

Marriages might be saved if someone invested in an adoptive family in such a way that they could provide appropriate childcare for the special needs involved. A midweek calibration might do wonders for a family on the edge and in need of intervention, because frontline ministries require reinforcements.

I had been reading to the kids about silkworms and metamorphosis, and was struck by this sentence:

> *"Once enclosed in its cocoon, the caterpillar withers and shrivels up, as if dying."* [1]

Cheerful, isn't it? Hang with me. Many mamas are right here, in the middle of the mess, shriveling in darkness. And we need to hear this.

> ***"It is an intermediate state*** *between the caterpillar and the butterfly. There can be seen certain projections which already indicate the shape of the future insect....Both the chrysalis and the nymph are insects* **in process of formation** *– insects closely wrapped in swaddling clothes, under which is finished the mysterious operation that will change their first structure from top to bottom."* [2]

Did you know that swaddling clothes are death wrappings? The same cloths wrapped around Jesus at birth were meant for wrapping around a dead body. But the same death that was meant to be the end of everything was actually the beginning that conquered death forever.

It is an intermediate state, this darkness. It is the space between two joys.

> *"It must get out of the cocoon. But how? The caterpillar has made the cocoon so solid and the butterfly is so weak! ...It would not be worth the trouble of going through so much to stifle miserably in the close cell, just as the end is attained!"*
>
> *"Could it not tear the cocoon open with its teeth?" asked Emile.*
>
> *"But, my innocent child, it has none, nor anything like them. It has only a proboscis, incapable of the slightest effort."*
>
> *"With its claws then?" suggested Jules.*
>
> *"Yes, if it had any strong enough. The trouble is, it is not provided with any."*
>
> *"But it must be able to get out," persisted Jules.*
>
> *"Doubtless it will get out.* **Has not every creature resources in the difficult moments of life!** *....But you would never guess the singular tool that it will use."* [3]

Tell me. Tell me how we stop the leak, refill, keep our kids safe, and protect our own oxygen level all at once. Tell me how we get from the new normal that feels like death and darkness to a new normal that feels like flying.

Ready?

> *"Insects' eyes are covered with a cap of transparent horn, hard and cut in facets. A magnifying glass is needed in order to distinguish these facets, they are so fine; but, fine as they are, they*

*have sharp bones which all together can, in time of need, be used as a grater...One by one the threads of silk succumb to the rasping. The hole is made, the butterfly comes out. What do you think about it? ...**Which of us would have thought of forcing the prison walls by striking them with the eye?**"*

– Jean Henri Fabre [4]

The Holy Spirit says, *Look at Me, Love. Your oxygen is right here. There's not much that prayer, education, and worship won't round out again.*

We are so busy looking at the darkness, and the darkness tries to command our attention. But we are not at the mercy of it because how we aim our vision is how we let the light break through.

> *Your eye is the lamp of your body. When your eye is healthy, your whole body is full of light, but when it is bad, your body is full of darkness.*
>
> *– Luke 11:34*

We're meant to thrive and grow, not just barely make it before our rims start wearing against the pavement. Which of us would have thought our freedom depended on what we focused our eyes on? Only the Creator who made a way for each of us to escape the darkness.

Look at Me, Love. This is how you walk on water, regardless of the waves and the wind.

It's hard, yes. Diagnoses and pain are real, and changing our focus doesn't change the past. It doesn't change Fetal Alcohol Syndrome, the amount of your paycheck, or the dysfunction of someone else.

But it's not the end. The prison turns into a place of new birth, oxygen changes our structure from top to bottom, and where we were earth-bound and vulnerable, we become strong and beautiful. It starts with looking at the One who fills us.

Another thing He revealed to me is that all of my longings – all the things I couldn't do because I was the mother of kids with so many special needs – had made me feel like I was somehow in disagreement with God, as though I wanted things for myself and my family that He didn't want for me. Because if He wanted them for me, they wouldn't be so impossible, right? We couldn't be in small groups. We couldn't take our kids to social functions (or any functions) without risking major upheaval. I couldn't finish projects on time and my husband couldn't quit his job because we needed the insurance to pay for medical issues. We couldn't go out on dates and we couldn't host ministry meetings in our home.

What the Lord showed me is that for the most part, He wanted all those things for me, too – just not yet, because this was the time of preparation for those things, and many others.

Andrey had his blood draw to screen for the genetic disorder, and it came back negative, praise God. Our house was even more overcrowded with seven kids in a three-bedroom house, and our hunt for a bigger space and new walls where we could build fresh memories began in earnest. But that's a different story.

This story, though, continued for a long time. Really, really hard behaviors continued for years with back and forth regression; someone ruined three mattresses in two years, and the effects of trauma on everyone began to show themselves. So I would not want you to read this far and think, *Sooo, they adopted and it was hard, she was miserable, but then she had a baby...and it was all better? Huh.* Because it was not all better. The waves still beat against us and the wind still blew. But my heart was better, and the vortex no longer sucked me under.

> *I am a frayed and nibbled survivor in a fallen world, and I am getting along. I am aging and eaten and have done my share of eating too. I am not washed and beautiful, in control of a shining world in which everything fits, but instead am wandering awed about on a splintering wreck I've come to care for, whose gnawed trees breathe delicate air, whose bloodied and scarred creatures are my dearest companions, and whose beauty beats and shines not in its imperfections but overwhelmingly in spite of them, under the wind-rent clouds, upstream and down.*

- Annie Dillard [5]

We can do hard things. Had I known what our family would walk through, I might've backed out.

I know it sounds terrible. I've heard virtuous-sounding adoptive parents repeatedly say, "I'd do it all over again," but I don't think I'm one of them. Those people are either better than me, stronger than me, or haven't come close to what we've gone through. And I'm okay with any of those options; this isn't a competition. The always-rainbows-and-sunshine blogs do a disservice to adoptive, foster, and special needs families, and I've been as honest with you here as I could while still trying to protect our privacy.

In the last eleven years I have faced deep fears I didn't even know existed. So many times, I was afraid one of our biological kids wouldn't make it through those years. So many times, I was afraid one of our adopted kids wouldn't make it very far into their future years. And there was that one season when I almost didn't make it, and it was years before it felt distant enough to confess. It's been a slow unfolding, because I needed to understand it first.

Don't ever stop praying for your adoptive and special needs friends. The contrast of discouragement and hope is violent, and when the next shoe keeps dropping (and how many shoes could there possibly be, anyway?) we have a hard time seeing goodness and light. It's a dangerous time to start agreeing with the enemy in despair, doubt, and fear, and if you have a friend in that place, they will almost never tell you how truly dark those darkest days are.

> *I think it's okay to take a long time to recover from seasons. After a while, they become part of our story and we seem to be able to integrate them. We can talk about them without too many automatic reactions going on and we can even write about them.*
>
> *But that doesn't mean we're completely recovered. I'm now kinder to myself. I treat myself with more grace. If I find that I'm overreacting to a threatening situation, I take time to think about where I've been. And I remember that the Lord has been with me.*

– Naomi Reed [6]

We wanted to be His hands and feet to these kids, but we had no idea how much we would need the rest of the body's support to be His hands and feet to us. And by the time we started to figure it out, it seemed like it was too late. But it's never too late, even if you still have years of hard things to walk through.

When we refer to people as the "hands and feet of Jesus" what we really mean is that these people saw something that most people didn't notice, and then they acted on it. Usually we think of it as service to others. Often, that service is preceded by investment in one's personal growth – hours spent studying or practicing a skill so we have more to leverage for the Kingdom. But sometimes we don't have that much time to prepare. And sometimes our preparation doesn't even come close to what is actually needed.

Hands and feet are helpless without the rest of the body. We needed people to notice us, so we could take turns being hands and feet. Sometimes we are the doers, other times we support others as they do the doing.

> *After the reading from the Law and the Prophets, the rulers of the synagogue sent a message to them, saying,* **"Brothers, if you have any word of encouragement for the people, say it."**
>
> – Acts 13:15

And now in these calmer days, He calls us to push these issues, bringing awareness and support. I'm convinced that many of the problems adoptive parents face are a direct result of adoption "advocacy" done by those who consider themselves experts but have never actually experienced what they're talking about.

We move one step forward, one step back, just like our kids, because almost every major step forward is met with spiritual attack. Often that attack manifests in some misbehavior, so the very thing people think we are now experts in can still make us feel like failures. It keeps us humble, so there's no danger of getting comfortable on a pedestal. So we, too, go back and forth in tentative steps: *I can't take it anymore,* and we try to retreat...but there is no retreating in the Kingdom when God has called you to obedience. And He has.

But what if our current struggle isn't the end game, because there's birth ahead? He never lets up in calling us to do the next brave thing. He is always about birthing victory and wholeness.

Whether the hard things were caused by our own choices, or those of others, or something completely unexplainable (because if we've learned anything from Job, it is that we don't want to be the ones who try to explain away everything), suffering combined with humility is the long view that includes hope and blessing at the end.

> *Those who live without fear are the most free and powerful people on earth. There is nothing that strikes more fear into the camp of the enemy than such a people walking the earth again.*
>
> – Rick Joyner [7]

The narrowing of the path makes the victory more acute – it becomes a bullseye, of sorts, to our breakthrough. And if we can get to that after conquering the darkness, there's no telling how many more victories are still to come.

One Sunday morning that summer, I drove with my left hand on the steering wheel while I ate chunks of watermelon with my right hand, the fork untouched on the seat next to me. The Stagecoach was full and loud music escaped the open windows as we drove a newly paved road through old woods on the way to church. "Stray Cat Strut" faded to "A Girl Named Tennessee," and the sun was brilliant on billions of green leaves.

It felt free and new and brave, the fresh air and loud music and watermelon juice on sticky fingers, with sunlight everywhere after such a dark season.

Friends, we have come a long way, but we still have a long way to go. We have not arrived. But I am finally, fully, and completely confident that someday we will.

In the dark place, in the fear, in the threat, in the life event that changes everything, we ask, *Is this going to be the end?* The waves are high, the wind is fierce. We feel the spray in our face as our feet grip the water, nothing else to hold onto.

And He answers, *No, Love. Eyes on Me. This is going to be your finest hour…so far.*

postscript

the cost: a challenge to adoption agencies, from the families who are living it

Thirty-seven thousand dollars. That's how much it cost to adopt two of our children.

And that was – forgive me – a screaming deal. We adopted them at the same time, from the same country, on one adoption fee instead of two separate fees. Many adoptions cost that much just for one child.

Talking about the numbers and the money bothers me because children are not commodities. Ignorant people joke to adoptive families about buying or selling children, revealing their cluelessness about the reality of child trafficking. Adoption expenses are not a sale; it's more like ransom money to get children out of institutions where they are languishing so they can be put into a family where they can heal.

And if you've adopted or read this book, you already know. Healing can take a long time, and healing is worth it.

But here's why I'm bringing up the money and numbers: Those costs do not come close to the ones incurred after adoption, literally and metaphorically. And people need to know that. People making insensitive jokes need to know; people thinking adoptive families get paid (what the what?!) need to know. And yes, potentially adoptive families need to know.

In discussing all the adoption costs with different agencies, it was never even recommended that we save for therapy. Personal health insurance was required, yes, but that doesn't begin to cover the entire costs of counseling for multiple people in a family – parents, adoptive children, biological children – who undergo the turmoil, trauma, and secondary trauma those early adoptive years often involve. When you are replacing or repairing damaged necessities every six months for the first two years, the co-pay for therapy – if therapy is even covered by your insurance – becomes out of the question since it's not a basic need.

We applied thousands of dollars to our international travel expenses. Hundreds of dollars were set aside to be converted to euro and lev just for meals. But also, it would have been good if we knew to set aside an account for therapy — $3000 to $5000 would have been a good start.

Why don't adoption agencies require or recommend this? I mentioned it to a friend, and her response was, "They'll never do it. Adoption agencies are making a sale, not equipping people for life after adoption."

It sounds jaded, but from my experience I have to agree with her. Are we wrong? I hope adoption agencies will prove it.

It's not just adoption agencies, though. Friends who adopted through both foster care and private adoption said this:

> *NO ONE PREPARED US. And we know they knew. Other families were and are our saving grace in this area of support.*
>
> *It would have taken just one home study writer or one agency worker thirty minutes to give us the real low down, and no one ever did.*

I contacted our adoption agency three times about *Upside Down* after it sold thousands of copies and gained the merit of being featured on Focus on the Family. I told them we hear from adoptive families all the time. Most of these families are desperate, and almost all of them tell us that *Upside Down* has the information they wish they had before they adopted. So I asked our adoption agency to consider making it one of their required (or at the very least, recommended) materials.

Why did I contact them three times? Because I never heard back. Not once.

We adopted two children with that agency. *We are one of their families.* And I never heard back. A few years later I tried again. This time there were a few emails back and forth, and they had someone on a committee review the book, and then…crickets. No returned email, no returned phone calls.

Maybe my friend is right. Maybe they are more interested in the sale than in equipping families. Maybe they are afraid of scaring people off. Maybe, after the obligatory first two years of intrusive home visits by a 20-something social worker whose sole parenting experience was with her biological toddler in a two-income family, they figured we'd consumed the entire plethora of support they offered and we were on our own at that point.

But here's the thing: If a family is easily scared off after reading a 100-page book or being told that part of the requirement for adoption is to save a few thousand dollars in an account for future counseling, those families should not be adopting in the first place. This is an easy filter.

Meanwhile, though, what can we do for adoptive families now? How can we encourage and empower them, and help them toward wholeness? What can we offer to potential adoptive families who are rightly curious about what they might be signing up for?

We can be honest with them, because what we've learned hasn't come cheap. We can be as transparent as possible while still honoring the privacy of our kids and families.

The core of adoption support is not going to come from professionals who don't have personal adoption experience. Those services are basic and they can help, but the most impactful support to adoptive families is going to come from other adoptive families who have traveled the same hard path. If that weren't the case, one of the most common things we hear from adoptive families wouldn't be "I would never tell this to someone who hasn't adopted, but I know you understand."

But that *is* what we hear, because we do understand. All these years later, we're still walking this out every day.

We need people who have been where we are – and are still walking that road – to come alongside us and say, *You're not alone. You're right, you really do know what you're talking about, even when you feel too ill-equipped to do this. This is really hard, but we're going to get through it.*

And that's cheaper than therapy.

endnotes

chapter 1
1. Shannon Guerra, *Upside Down: Understanding and Supporting Attachment in Adoptive and Foster Families* (Wasilla, Alaska: Copperlight Wood, 2019), 1.

chapter 2
1. Natasha Metzler, "To the Adoptive Mom Struggling to Love Her Traumatized Child," https://natashametzler.com/to-the-adoptive-mom-struggling-to-love-her-traumatized-child/ (accessed February 7, 2022).

chapter 4
1. Katie Davis, *Kisses From Katie* (New York: Howard Books, 2011), 181.

chapter 5
1. C.S. Lewis, *The Silver Chair* (New York: HarperCollins, 1953), 22.
2. Ibid, 23.
3. Ibid.

chapter 7
1. H.E. Marshall, *This Country of Ours* , public domain.
2. L.M. Montgomery, *Anne of Green Gables* (New York: Bantam Books, 1987), 10.

chapter 8
1. C.S. Lewis, *Mere Christianity* (New York: MacMillan Publishing Company, 1952), 126.
2. Charlotte Mason, *Home Education* (Quarryville, Penn: Charlotte Mason Research and Supply, 1989), 96.

3. James Dobson, *Bringing Up Boys* (Wheaton, Ill: Tyndale, 2001), 84.
4. Benjamin Franklin, *The Autobiography of Benjamin Franklin* (New Haven: Yale University Press, 1964), 234.ocean

chapter 9
1. Karen Burton Mains, *Open Heart, Open Home* (Elgin, Ill.: David C. Cook Publishing Co., 1976), 41.
2. Ibid.
3. J.R.R. Tolkien, *The Two Towers* (New York: Houghton Mifflin Harcourt Publishing Company, 1966), 430.

chapter 10
1. Boris Gindis, "Post-Orphanage Behavior in Internationally Adopted Children," *Center for Cognitive-Developmental Assessment and Remediation,* http://www.bgcenter.com/BGPublications/OrphanageBehavior.htm (accessed 5/29/23).
2. Ibid.

chapter 11
1. A.A. Milne, *The Complete Tales and Poems of Winnie-the-Pooh* (New York: Anytime Books, 1996), 311-312.
2. Charles Dickens, *Bleak House* (New York: Books Inc., undated copyright), 401.
3. Charlotte Mason, *Home Education* (Quarryville, Penn: Charlotte Mason Research and Supply, 1989), 194-195.

chapter 12
1. Charlotte Mason, *Home Education* (Quarryville, Penn: Charlotte Mason Research and Supply, 1989).
2. Louisa May Alcott, *Little Women* (Philadelphia, Penn: Running Press, 1995), 577.
3. Ibid, 595.
4. Charlotte Mason, *Home Education* (Quarryville, Penn: Charlotte Mason Research and Supply, 1989), 263.

chapter 13
1. C.S. Lewis, *The Last Battle* (New York: HarperCollins, 1956), 210-211.
2. C.S. Lewis, *The Lion, The Witch, and The Wardrobe* (New York: HarperCollins, 1950), 158.
3. Charles Kingsley, *The Heroes* (1889), public domain.

chapter 14
1. J.R.R. Tolkien, *The Fellowship of the Ring* (New York: Houghton Mifflin Harcourt Publishing Company, 1966), 339.
2. Elizabeth Prentiss, *Stepping Heavenward* (Ulrichsville, Ohio: Barbour Publishing Inc., 1998), 164-165.

chapter 15
1. J.R.R. Tolkien, *The Fellowship of the Ring* (New York: Houghton Mifflin Harcourt Publishing Company, 1966), 50.
2. Ibid, 87.
3. Ibid, 267.
4. J.R.R. Tolkien, *The Two Towers* (New York: Houghton Mifflin Harcourt Publishing Company, 1966), 696.

chapter 16
1. *God Calling*, ed. A.J. Russell (Ulrichsville, Ohio: Barbour Publishing, 1998), entry titled "April 17."

chapter 17
1. Annie Dillard, *Pilgrim at Tinker Creek* (New York: HarperPerennial: 1974), 75.

chapter 18
1. Jan Karon, *Somewhere Safe With Somebody Good* (New York: Putnam, 2014), 226.
2. Lisa Bevere, *Girls With Swords* (Colorado Springs: Waterbrook Press, 2013), 100-101.
3. Annie Dillard, *Pilgrim at Tinker Creek* (New York: HarperPerennial: 1974).

chapter 19

1. Fabre, *The Storybook of Science* (Chapel Hill, NC: Yesterday's Classics, 2006), 112.

2. Ibid.

3. Ibid, 113-114.

4. Ibid, 114.

5. Annie Dillard, *Pilgrim at Tinker Creek* (New York: HarperPerennial: 1974), 245.

6. Naomi Reed, *My Seventh Monsoon* (Crown Hill, Milton Keynes: Authentic Media Ltd., 2011), 144.

7. Rick Joyner, "The Warrior Nation--The New Church Leadership," *The Elijah List,* http://www.elijahlist.com/words/display_word/4222 (accessed July 31, 2023).

acknowledgments

To my early readers and reviewers: Thank you for your honest feedback, questions, experience, and mad proofreading skillz. Thank you especially to Leslie and Sarah for reviewing a touchy part (when it was still badly written, even) and giving validation, empathy, and a thumbs-up to it.

To our various church families: Thank you for being humble and teachable as you have welcomed us and chosen to learn and walk alongside us.

To dear friends who were alluded to or quoted but left unnamed in these chapters to maintain privacy and keep people guessing: Jess, Wendy, Amanda, Sarah, Jen...your years of friendship, prayers, and understanding have bouyed our family. Some of you know the watery path and it is an honor to be with you on it.

To Vincent, Iree, Afton, Chamberlain, Andrey, Reagan, Finnegan, and Kavanagh: Thank you for living through this with us. You all have rolled with major life changes and continue to live with the consequences, both good and hard. In the face of attack and difficulty, each of you have forged strength and maturity, and I am so proud of you.

To Vince, thank you for living this life with me. Thank you for giving me extra hours at the computer, and extra hours of prayer and processing on the couch, and for quietly leaving coffee on my desk when I was in the zone or in tears. There's nobody I'd rather risk the ocean with.

To God the Father, Jesus, and Holy Spirit: You are the love triumphant. You always win. Thank You for grace and forgiveness and second chances. Thank You for inviting us out of the boat, for teaching us when to rock it, and for

showing us that we will never be overwhelmed by the water or alone as we walk on it.

*When you pass through the waters, I will be with you;
and through the rivers, they shall not overwhelm you;
when you walk through fire you shall not be burned,
and the flame shall not consume you.*

– Isaiah 43:2

also by Shannon Guerra

"What makes this book stand out from other contemporary Christian writings on prayer is the author's crisp prose and sharp sense of humor. . .
An insightful, honest, and genuinely funny author delivers a standout devotional." – *Kirkus Reviews*

Companion Journal and Study Guide also available.

Adoptive and foster families often feel alone, but it doesn't have to be that way. Shannon Guerra learned this first-hand after she and her husband adopted two children in 2012, and she started writing shockingly transparent blog posts about what her family was going through at home, at the doctor's office, and in her heart as a mama.

And then adoptive and foster families started writing back. Their overwhelming, unanimous theme was, "This is what I've wanted to tell people for so long. **I wish everyone who knows our family could read this."**

Upside Down is the result. Because adoptive and foster families should never feel alone, and communities can be equipped to make sure they never feel that way again.

Moms, you pour yourselves out every day. How about some powerful refilling, in doable doses?

Short chapters. White space. Deep-down hope, and out-loud laughter.

Work That God Sees is 285 (ish, who's counting) pages of powerful refilling in doable doses: encouragement, easy recipes, mom hacks, wisdom, a few crafty patterns and tons of roaring hilarity. Also included are questions for personal journaling or small group discussion and several lessons you can learn at someone else's expense. But watch out for the cayenne pepper – don't say I didn't warn you.

ABIDE is a different kind of devotional: A 6-volume series of fully illustrated books that are part devotional, part coffee table book, part magazine. These beautiful books will lead you further into the presence of God as you grow deep and wide, pressing forward in these seasons that stretch us. Each is roughly 70-80 pages, containing full color photographs, a light-yoked study section for personal or small group use, an extra recipe or two, and powerful encouragement that meets you where you're at and moves you toward breakthrough.

Titles:

Rest in the Running
Hope in the Waiting
Clarity in the Longing
Bravery for the Next Step
Obedience to Move Forward
Surrendering to Win

one more thing...

Need more encouragement for the season you're in? Do you want to grow deep and wide, regardless of your space and circumstances?

You are warmly invited to **shannonguerra.com** where I'm transparent about finding peace in the hard moments, beauty in the mess, and white space in the chaos.

If you want, you can sign up for new posts and monthly newsletters, straight to your inbox – they are spamless, occasionally brilliant and/or hilarious, and never leave the toilet seat up, talk back, or claw your furniture.

Bring a cup of tea or coffee and curl up at your leisure... or just lock yourself in the bathroom for a few minutes with some chocolate. That's what I do.

His peace is for you,

Shannon Guerra

website: www.shannonguerra.com
subscribe: www.shannonguerra.substack.com

www.ingramcontent.com/pod-product-compliance
Lightning Source LLC
Chambersburg PA
CBHW031102080526
44587CB00011B/787